CW01418419

To: MAIRI

FROM ONE TEACHER
TO ANOTHER!

ALL THE BEST

DAVID
10 SEP 2017

WHAT HE SEES IS WHAT YOU GET

MARTIAL ARTS TRAINING THROUGH THE TEACHER'S EYES

GM
DAVID J.
HARRELL

Matador
9 Priory Business Park,
Wistow Road, Kibworth Beauchamp,
Leicestershire. LE8 0RX
Tel: 0116 279 2299
Email: books@troubador.co.uk
Web: www.troubador.co.uk/matador
Twitter: @matadorbooks

ISBN 978 1785893 681

British Library Cataloguing in Publication Data.
A catalogue record for this book is available from the British Library.

Printed and bound by CPI Group (UK) Ltd, Croydon, CR0 4YY
Typeset in 11pt Adobe Garamond Pro by Troubador Publishing Ltd, Leicester, UK

Matador is an imprint of Troubador Publishing Ltd

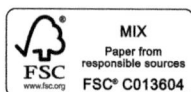

MIX
Paper from
responsible sources
FSC
www.fsc.org
FSC® C013604

This book is dedicated to the memory of my beloved parents, David J. and Mary T. Harrell. Without their foresight and concern for my personal development, I would not have been introduced to the wonderful world of classic martial art training.

I probably would have become a totally different person and would never have had the privilege of enjoying the pleasures and challenges martial training can bring into one's life or the opportunity to share knowledge that can lead to personal development.

WHAT HE SEES IS WHAT YOU GET

TABLE OF CONTENTS

Part One: The Early Years

Part Two: Teaching

Part Three: Applying Lessons Learned

ACKNOWLEDGEMENTS

First and foremost, all praise and thanks be to God. It is by his lead that all things are accomplished and made possible. I give thanks for the opportunities he has blessed me with and I pray that this book serves as a helpful and useful tool.

I would like to dedicate this book to my teachers for their unselfish, uncompromising willingness to share with me their expert knowledge and illuminating views on the martial arts. I would like to express my deep appreciation and indebtedness in particular to the following:

Hanshi Frank Hargrove PhD, Grand Master Jung Un Lee, Grand Master Duk Gun Kwon PhD, Grand Master Hae Man Park, and to my first teacher, Grand Master Harold Lee Hankins (deceased).

I want to thank my wife, Nicky, my sons, Isaiah, Amoz and Imran, my father-in-law, Rennie Cameron and the rest of my family, who supported and encouraged me in spite of all the time it took me away from them. It was a long and difficult journey for them.

I would also like to thank Master Margaret Evans who provided support, talked things over, read, wrote, offered comments, allowed me to quote her remarks, and assisted in the process of selection, editing, proofreading and design.

I would like to express my gratitude to: GM Zeyad Hammad Abu Zahieh, GM Khalil Jabran, GM Leon Preston, GM Jay Dunston, GM Jack Dark, GM Hassan Iskandar, GM Sterling Chase, GM Charles January, Master Norbert Amefu and Master Shivram Makwana. Without your collective insistence that I write down my martial art understanding and thoughts, this book would never have found its way to the publisher.

Thanks are also due to Sifu Bruce Clark, the first martial artist I met when I moved to Aberdeen. His continued friendship I will forever value.

I would also like to express my gratitude to Zaman Awan at the Golden Tulip Hotel Sharjah, United Arab Emirates, where I completed this book, for the warm, friendly and convenient accommodation.

Last but not least: I beg forgiveness of all those who have been with me over the course of the years and whose names I have failed to mention.

FOREWORD

GM David J. Harrell's expertise is most evident when he is sharing, questioning, exploring, researching and examining today's martial arts instruction, the past generation's methods and its sporting counterpart. With his progressive manner, GM David rarely accepts a martial input from any source without asking for its historical characteristics or evaluating its consequential effects on his students. For him the past and present are vital indicators of what can happen in the future.

In his first book, GM David shares his growth as a person, his martial arts training background and his research efforts. He also addresses the many aspects of traditional martial arts training that are beneficial, in spite of a declining interest in the sport.

For example, sports competitions in Taekwondo have become so elite with their sporting demands that components of personal improvement have been underdeveloped or overlooked altogether. Historically, martial arts training provided the typical practitioners with a path to better fitness levels, at the same time offering self-empowering and effective self-protection elements. Attributes linked with spiritual development were also included.

GM David's classic martial arts instructional skills will

appeal to people of all age groups who are seeking personal growth. His analysis of teaching methods and approaches invites the reader to look for the next step in the evolution of the practice, and promises to enchant anyone who has ever questioned the inherent personal benefits in classical martial art training.

Grand Master Albert Cheeks, *9th Degree Black Belt*
President of Ki Whang Kim Martial Arts Association
Member of the Taekwondo Hall Fame

PREFACE

This book is about my attempts to make a contribution to a profession whose daily efforts and challenges affect the global population. That profession is teaching. More specifically, embedded in these few pages is the story of the making of a teacher who has dedicated most of his life to the study and practice of an ancient art of self-defence, and to understanding how the applications of its technical principles and its philosophical ideology is able to reshape lives for the good of humanity.

On December 25, 2012, while sitting in my room at the Holiday Inn International Sharjah United Arab Emirates, I wrote:

> *One of the most exciting, satisfying and rewarding situations to have, opportunities to be blessed with, or professions to enter, is the teaching role. Teaching someone how to ride a bike, sing a song, speak a language, drive a car, play a sport, dance to a tune, use a computer, fly an airplane, to become a surgeon, to climb mountains, how to think.*

What an amazing gift to possess!

Have you ever wondered what was inside the mind of a teacher?

Being a teacher is not confined to a select group or class of individuals, every human being is a teacher with varying levels of skills in a variety of subjects. During the course of a lifespan everyone on the face of the Earth will have taught someone something!

The teachers I identify with and admire are the real teachers, those who have chosen to dedicate their lives to the art of teaching.

I believe that the mindset behind the teaching process is elementary. Irrespective of the subject, the activity or the arena for deployment, the mind's eye of the teacher remains consistently true, it sees what it sees – and responds accordingly. It lacks borders or boundaries. I liken it to an artist painting a portrait, inspired by the intangible, the unseen.

This is the sphere of teaching into which I proposed to venture many years ago when I asked my first and every subsequent martial art teacher to teach me to teach the art to others.

"Can you see what I see?"

Teaching is the only profession to which every person has been exposed at some stage in their life, as everyone has been a student. But do you really know what teachers do, where teachers work, and what kind of teachers there are? Teachers have wide and varied responsibilities including:

- teaching students of different ages and abilities
- preparing lessons and teaching materials
- marking and assessing work

- organizing displays in the classroom
- liaising with non-teaching staff such as teacher aides and therapists
- discussing student progress with parents and guardians
- working with colleagues and in professional teams
- organizing excursions, school performances and sporting events
- supervising extra-curricular activities
- attending meetings and professional development classes.

Teachers work in many different types of schools and educational settings including:

- primary schools
- secondary schools
- schools of excellence (both academic and sport)
- special-needs schools
- hospital schools
- centres for sport and recreational development
- outdoor and environmental education centres
- youth training and education centres
- correctional facilities (youth and adult).

I anticipate that most of the people who have been curious enough to pick up this book will be martial artists, some will be instructors like myself. Haven't you given lessons in a variety of venues? Haven't you found there is a whole lot more to teaching than standing in front of a class giving instructions? Would you have thought that you were a teacher not unlike those you will find in classrooms all over the world, teaching our children? There are many different types of teachers. Most teachers choose a specialist area because they like working with children of a particular age group or because they have a passionate love of a specific subject area.

This book is about the methods I use to teach martial arts to children and adults at the Traditional Martial Arts Institute (the Institute). It includes subjective input from the parents of some of my students, and from students past and present.

Some names have been changed to protect privacy.

PART ONE

THE EARLY YEARS

THE BEGINNING

My journey started in the segregated south-eastern section of the United States – in Virginia, the Confederate Capital.

There are two things I always wanted to be: an engineer who designed (since the age of six) and a martial arts teacher.

At the beginning of any project, I was able to see not only the finished project, but also all of the steps and stages necessary to achieve the completed product. Even the finest details were vividly clear in my mind's eye. As time went on, and to the present day, this God-given ability became revered and sought after in the form of advice. People thought that I could predict whether or not a venture would be successful and suggest planning improvements, if necessary, to ensure the success of their project.

This ability was regarded as 'weird' by my peers. However, looking back, I can see that they were the skills that I later used to become a successful project manager. I did not have to be taught them; they just came naturally to me. These same skills were also invaluable in my journey to become a teacher of the martial arts. My very first design was a doghouse for a pup I had found in the woods. My father refused to assist me with its construction until I had produced a sketch with outlined dimensions and a list of building materials. My electrical design career included nuclear-powered submarines and aircraft carriers, a variety of surface military aircraft, nuclear power plants and finally the aerospace industry.

Success in the design world was the vehicle that supported all my financial needs, served as a platform for social status recognition and stabilized my mental self-worth needs in a racially charged period of American history.

Parallel to my professional career, my martial arts training and development shared an equal yet quiet success. My ability to visualize a successful end product and understand in detail how that successful outcome could be achieved also contributed to my martial art teaching. For example, I can watch a champion fighter's moves and kicks and understand how he was taught to execute those moves. I can visualize the drills that had to be put in place in order to perfect the fighter's techniques. What this means is that I can then teach my student the antidote to those techniques so that he/she is able to defend against them. If the student understands and is able to perform the defence against a technique, he/she is also more able to execute the technique itself and therefore able to beat that particular opponent.

All of my martial arts teachers have one thing in common: I asked each one of them to teach me to teach!

They were very good teachers. They were also very good students. I often wondered if they had been taught to teach or whether their teachers were simply masters of the art of teaching. What is clear to me today is that there are two qualities that are essential in order to be an effective teacher:

- knowledge of the content
- the ability to communicate it

- Knowing the material is not enough to be effective in teaching it! So my teachers obviously had another thing in common: they all possessed these two qualities

I am the type of martial artist that constantly reassesses myself. Seeking self-knowledge in relation to areas of strength helps me to recognize achievement and to challenge underachievement. I try to instill in my students this same approach to their martial art and to their day-to-day lives. I have been taught to constantly challenge myself to improve my skills so that I can deliver the goods.

I just want to get it right!

I just don't want to leave out any ingredients from the recipe that has been handed down to me.

My students deserve my best. I want to be the teacher that is sought after.

After all, a teacher's purpose is not to create students in his / her own image, but to develop students who can create their own image.

FIGHTING THROUGH CHILDHOOD

I was born in Suffolk, Virginia, the eldest of the three boys of David and Mary Thelma Harrell. I started my martial art training at the age of twelve. I think that my dad understood that martial art training was something that I needed to do to curb my temper. Dad worked in the naval shipyard and, of course, whilst working there he met sailors who had travelled all over the world. Whilst talking to one of these sailors, Dad mentioned me and said that I had a real bad temper and that he needed to do something about it. He knew that I had academic potential, but he realized that my instinct to fight my way out of every situation meant that I was going nowhere fast.

The sailor suggested that I needed to develop self-discipline and that martial art training would help me to do that. He said that my temper was part of my nature and that this could not be changed through martial art training, however I could learn to control it. Through the training I would learn to identify those things that triggered my temper so that I could avoid them.

Why did I fight so much? To answer that, I need to paint a picture of what life was like for me as a child. As far back as I can remember, I have suffered from asthma. Not only was I asthmatic, but I was also allergic to almost everything under the sun. In fact, I was probably even allergic to the sun. I was certainly allergic to cows' milk and was raised on goats' milk. My arm looked like a pincushion from all of the injections I needed. During my primary school days, I was constantly ill with one thing or another. Because I lived in the southeast, the climate was very damp. In the summer it was humid as hell and in the winter it was cold and damp and not good for my health. To make matters worse, I had every childhood disease you can name! As a result, I spent a lot of my youth looking out of my bedroom window because I was too ill to go outside to play like my brothers.

I was a skinny, frail kid who had very little to say. When I did go outside, I was subject to bullying! Despite my allergies and illness, however, I had a secret: I was a fighter. That is what sickness and hard times often produces. And my tool was boxing. My father had boxed while serving in the armed forces. So he taught his three sons the tricks of the trade. Any bully who attacked me was met with a surprise fist-attack that he never forgot. A bully only bullied me once and this quiet, sickly-looking boy learned to express himself with his fists. I just would not tolerate what I regarded as foolishness so I fought back. I would just simply fight back, and it didn't take much! By the time I reached my teens, I had established a reputation that overshadowed my academic potential.

Although I was angry or had a chip on my shoulder, I don't know where it came from, or why. I think that all of my generation was angry. We had to be angry inside seeing the realities of everyday life for our parents at the height of segregation. I think that the Black Movement was a result of kids like me who had grown up and were frustrated, angry and sick of it. Unfortunately, the only people I was fighting were my own people, blacks, and ignorant ones at that!

By the summer of 1962 I was nearly thirteen years old. My health had improved to the point that I was playing more outdoors and had begun to take an interest in baseball. I recall playing it every day, weather permitting. I wasn't very good at it. My eye–hand coordination was poor. Due to the fact that I spent my early years indoors suffering with asthma, my motor skills were not as developed as they should have been. In fact, I was very clumsy and more often than not, I could not catch very well. I still enjoyed playing the game though.

The neighborhood boys club invited a martial arts guy to do a demonstration one Saturday afternoon. I found it fascinating! The high kicks and punches left me spellbound for weeks after. I wasn't the only one to be captivated as I remember that there were two other kids who found the demonstration impressive as well. The three of us started to practise together, making up moves as we went along. One of the boys found a book written by Ohae Konakoki and read it from cover to cover.

Another discovery for us was *Black Belt Magazine* and we did the same with this, absorbing its contents eagerly. The guy who gave the original demonstration continued to come on Saturdays, offering free instruction to whoever showed up. I was right there, sucking in everything he taught. It was very elementary, though. I did not start to get formal training until I met Grand Master Harold Hankins in the late 1960s.

MY FIRST MARTIAL ART TEACHER

Mama and Daddy had found out martial art training was good for my temperament and my health too. Encouraged by this piece of information about martial art training, they supported my search for a school. Mr Hankins was the only local choice. I say 'local' but his dojo was in the city of Norfolk, some thirty-odd miles away, and training cost $25 per month.

Mr Hankins was learning too, and he had to go all the way to Silver Springs, Maryland to study under Grand Master Ki Whang Kim because no one in Virginia would teach blacks. One reason was that integration was still foreign to the locals and most karate schools were in white areas of town. Another reason was that Asian instructors were of the opinion that 'colored' people (as we were called back then), were too stupid to learn martial arts or were too poor to pay for lessons. Another fear was that they would lose their white clients if 'colored' people were in the same room. Where would we have gone to learn martial arts? You know, the moment you walked into the school, the guy would think you were just going to clean the floor for him. He certainly was not going to teach you martial arts.

What a teacher Mr Hankins was! He was articulate, smart, big, very black in complexion, and he feared no man! It was he who taught me how to kick and punch like a machine. He put the 'C' in conditioning and made us physically fit. He truly epitomized the tenets of Taekwondo, being upright in every way, a role model for his students of every age. If there are any individuals that I have ever feared, but also admired and looked up to, they were my father and Mr Hankins.

In a word, all of Mr Hankins' students were noted for one thing – fearlessness! His teaching came directly from GM Ki Whang Kim of Silver Springs, Maryland, a four-hour drive away. Mr Hankins would drive up on Friday after work to train on Friday night and all day Saturday with GM Kim. Maryland had been one of the so-called 'free states' wishing to abolish slavery. It had a known history of racial tolerance. It was under the direction of GM Kim that we got our weekly nurturing in Korean Karate, as it was known back then.

GM Kim was known for his spinning kick techniques. He had studied under Kanken Toyama whilst in Japan at Nihon University. Kanken Toyama was the founder of Shudokan karate. Back in Korea, GM Kim had been nicknamed 'the Typhoon'. GM Kim passed away on September 16, 1993 at the age of seventy-three.

Even today, the Institute, aka The House of Sweat, is known for its spinning kicks. It's in our roots! We were taught to fight whenever and wherever. One of my black belts recently completed an essay that asked what my brand of martial arts had taught him. His initial reply was 'How to fight!'

A typical Mr Hankins workout started with calisthenics, which included push-ups on the knuckles. He would actually walk around with a piece of paper that he would use to slide under the fist. This was to test that only two knuckles of the fist were on the floor. Oh! I forgot to mention the floor. The dojo, as it was called back then, was on the top floor of a four-story building known to locals as the Wood Street YMCA. Ironically, this building in 1934 was the first site of Norfolk State College.

Being an old building in a colored neighborhood meant it had no elevator, so climbing those stairs for each class got you fit real quick. Once at the top floor, a few steps and you were at the door. As you entered the room you would notice the three painted brick columns running from floor to ceiling and a concrete floor that had been painted black. There were windows the length of the building and newspapers stuffed in the glass where a stone had been thrown through it. In the wintertime you could see your breath with each word you uttered and you prayed for a big class that night to help heat up the room. Sitting quietly in a corner of the room was a makiwara. The makiwara is a padded striking post used as a tool to condition body parts such as the knuckles of the fist, the blade of the hand, the heel of the palm and the fingertips. Each working session with it left your hands swollen and your knuckles sore. Long before Sensei Hankins would appear, the floor had to be mopped, the windows cleaned and dusted or else there was hell to pay! It was part of the discipline imposed and the respect due to the instructor.

Each and every class began and ended with a call to attention, bowing to the flag and to the instructors. The Korean language was used and each new student was given a legal-sized piece of paper with Korean terms and phrases on both the front and back of it. He or she had two weeks to learn every word or there was a price to pay. After the calisthenics came blocking, punching and kicking drills, followed by Kata/hyungs or sometimes kumite (sparring) or bunkai, and finishing with the makiwara. Words like Poomsae, Sabum Nim, Gyoroogi, or Hoshin sool had not been created yet. It was mainly Japanese language-based with some Korean terms. Counting was done in Korean.

Back then we did not have paddles to kick. Instead, there was a pail of used X-ray sheets that we used as paddles. Mr Hankins' wife, Alfarces, was a nurse at the hospital so she kept us supplied with X-ray sheets. Sensei Hankins would hold a sheet up at face level and give the command to do a round kick. You knew your kicks were powerful if you were able to rip the sheet with one kick. While sparring, suffering an injury or experiencing pain was not a reason to quit. You did the drills until he told you to stop.

The early days were painful days and I was absolutely afraid of Mr Hankins, my first martial art teacher. I didn't realize at the time that he was passionate about martial art and about teaching it to us. It wasn't a game; it was real, which meant that it would be useful to us for the rest of our lives. Grand Master Jack Dark once said to me, "Do you know what, you sound just like Mr Hankins!" I said, "We probably all do." His excitement and the way he spoke when we got it right terrified us. We thought we had done something wrong, but that was how Mr Hankins was. He was excited that you got it right finally but at the same time, if you got it wrong he was equally as excitable. It would sound something like this:

"How many times have I got to tell you this? You weren't listening! You're not listening are you? You better find it!"

He was like that. So it was nerve-racking for me, but I

learned how to concentrate and focus so that I could get it right.

I learned from being at Mr Hankins' school that if I got angry I should keep it to myself because I wasn't going to win. It was in his class that I discovered what real fear was, because I could see what a guy could do to a body with his hands and his feet, or with his elbows or his knees. It's devastating, especially if his hands and feet have been conditioned on a makiwara: his hands and feet would go right through your body.

You take a lot of things for granted if you're training, like breaking with your fingertips or breaking with your head. The average person can't do that! Not only can you do it, you do it with the state of mind that you're going to run your hand through the person's body, so you're talking about a human weapon. That's the difference. You've been conditioned to use any part of your body and turn it into a projectile that will maim and kill. You know that the moment you execute it. When I realized how dangerous I could be, that was when I gained a sense of responsibility.

So I learned to hone my skills by practising with other students and sometimes I might get upset that the person had got me. I wasn't getting upset because he hurt me, but because he got me. I realized that, had he wanted to hurt me and got that punch in with the intent of hurting me, I wouldn't be standing. He just touched me hard. Maybe a little harder than I felt comfortable with or felt like it should be, but to get angry and say, "I'm going to get you back" – no! The first thing I learned from training with Mr Hankins was that someone who loses it – loses control of himself – cannot win. He just gets beaten worse.

One time in Mr Hankins' class there were two other guys from Suffolk. I remember the time when one of these guys accidentally challenged one of the black belt instructors. The misunderstood challenge took place while we were doing sparring drills. At the end of that sparring time the student said to the instructor, "Hey, let's go a little bit more." I can vividly recall the instructor looked at Mr Hankins and then he said "Okay," and Mr Hankins said, "Use control." The instructor put a round kick right upside the student's head and he dropped to the floor. His request to "Go a little bit more," was interpreted as "I think I can beat you". He didn't understand what the protocol was. What he should have said was "Can you practise with me a little bit more so I can get it right?" That's what the student meant, but it was perceived as a challenge.

We all learned a lesson at his expense. What we learned was that if you wanted to go a little extra there was a way of doing it, there was a protocol that you had to follow to do that. For example, "How did you do that, Sir?" or "Can you show me how you did that?" That's different from saying, "Hey, let's go some more."

We didn't get to choose who we sparred with. The instructor said, "You and you." Sometimes students could be heard making a gasping sound. That told us that it was going to be a good, entertaining battle. These guys would go at it. Then sometimes the instructor would choose one strong and one weaker student. We could see the horror in this kid's face because he knew he was going to get beaten, and weeks later he disappeared. We wouldn't see him again. He quit. Only the tough survived.

Given more time and training this guy would have been good. He just needed a little bit of nourishment, he needed a little bit more encouragement, he needed a little bit more confidence. He just needed more time to find himself and he was chased out by somebody who took advantage of another student's skills to a point that it intimated the other student. Everyone knew what was happening. The instructor knew it. This is the reason that I don't have sparring! I have sparring drills! This is because the drills allow everyone to develop a comfort-zone and a confidence in their skills without the hassle of me trying to control a student's development by avoiding contact with certain people who have better skills. That's equally as damaging in their confidence development. You lose students that way! Secondly, but more importantly, you don't give that person time to develop his or her own character.

The martial art I teach is the same martial art I was taught, but *the way I teach* can be different from *how I was taught*. I was the type of person who, if you beat me today, I would figure out what I did wrong so I could beat you tomorrow, but a lot of people don't think like that. There're so many people who would take that beating as a beating that they're going to weigh up for the rest of their life. They can't get past it. They could, in time, have had skills and confidence that would allow them a real chance against anybody they faced.

It was always a paradox. Which animal defends itself better, the lion or the turtle? It's all relative. A lion can't get into the turtle. It can kick the turtle around, or throw it around, and when it gets tired of doing what it's doing, it goes away upset. The turtle walks away happy that it sees another day. So who won the fight?

This is how I try to teach! I try to teach in such a fashion that it allows everyone a chance to develop. I've used this analogy many times: you go and buy yourself two rhododendron bushes, take them home and plant them. You plant them in the same area where they get the same amount of sunlight and give them the same treatments, nutrients or whatever else. Which one is going to blossom first? You don't know, and that's how it is with me. I give everyone the same nourishment and I just wait until they bloom at their own time under their own terms. That's growth! That's what growth really is in martial arts. I've just got to be patient and I've got to make sure that everything around is preserved to allow that to happen.

That's why I take it to heart when someone does quit or leaves for whatever reason. I didn't finish my job! I think that's what I get more disturbed about, but only because I can see what that person could be, but that person can't see it. I feel like I failed because the teacher's supposed to be able to teach in such a fashion that it allows that person to get a glimpse of what he or she might be able to be or might be able to achieve, and maybe I didn't do it.

I am often reminded of a story about a teacher of animals. He had a large collection of the various species that roamed the land and the sea. His collection was made up of the brightest and smartest of their kind. He frequently wondered how he could determine which was the smartest of all his creatures but could come to no firm conclusion. Eventually he came up with the idea of creating a test that would answer his question. What about a tree? Surely the one who could climb a tree the fastest must be the smartest!

So he proceeded to carry out the test. When the test was over, the fish spent the rest of his life wondering and regretting his stupidity, which had prevented him from carrying out such a simple task. Now, it is obvious that a fish is not equipped with the tools for climbing. So the fish was not a failure. The fault lay with the teacher who was unable to recognize and appreciate the unique talents and qualities of each individual and to create an equitable evaluation procedure that offered growth leading to empowerment. I do not want any student leaving my class thinking he or she is a failure because they are unable to perform jump, spinning kicks or flying side-kicks. Don't get me wrong! It is exciting to have students who have the ability to perform these techniques and I enjoy teaching them, but I am interested in the whole person, not just one aspect of the person. I try to build on the skills that each student has so that he or she can reach their own personal best. The qualities that I value and try to promote in students include respect for self and others, determination, perseverance, a sense of responsibility and a questioning mind.

In May 2013 I distributed a questionnaire to all of my black belt students. I asked them the following question:

"What has martial arts training taught me that has made a difference in my life, and how?"

Some of the responses surprised me, but all of them encouraged me to believe that my aim to give them skills that would be of value to them in all aspects of their lives was achieving good results. Changes identified by students included:

- the setting of goals and aspirations
- strength of mind and the ability to analyze problems and overcome obstacles and challenges

- ability to think logically
- improved self-esteem and self-confidence
- improved health and fitness and (for some) improvement in medical conditions
- improved school / work ethic.

I also asked them to try to explain how they thought their training had helped to bring about these changes. All of them made reference to the structure and discipline of the training. They all felt that this had helped them to work harder at school or to put more effort into their jobs.

All of the students spoke about the discipline associated with their training. They credited the structure and discipline with helping them to develop the self-discipline that enabled them to work harder at school. The demands on their bodies and minds that the hard physical workouts made had strengthened their desire to persevere in the face of adversity and disappointment. They had learned that the person who loses control has effectively beaten him/herself with the result that they now found it less difficult to master their emotions and not to let them overcome mental discipline. For younger, school-age students in particular, realizing that they could defend themselves against an aggressor had improved their self-confidence to the extent that they believed that they were more likely to walk away from an argument. In addition, their training had shown them the necessity of being alert and aware of their surroundings. This had been absorbed into their everyday lives so that they were able to anticipate and avoid confrontations.

Arduous tasks such as speaking in front of the class at school or responding to the boss's questions had become easier.

This was attributed to the belt grading process within the Traditional Taekwondo Institute, which involves writing an essay for each grading and discussing this in front of other students and spectators. They also ascribed some of the improvement in their ability to 'think' to being given an essay to write on topics or concepts and ideas which they had never really thought about in any depth. In some cases, the essay topic was a subject that they knew absolutely nothing about, forcing them to research the topic in order to be able to understand and explain it to an audience.

I did not ask the students to comment about my skills as an instructor but their responses clearly showed that they believed that the instructor should be a role model. The instructor whose attitude is 'do as I say, not as I do' may still be good at teaching them to kick and punch but he/she will never be able to inspire students to believe in themselves and their ability to have a positive influence on the world around them. One teenage student commented:

"In life you have to do things you don't want to do, but if you persevere and set your mind you can do anything!"

Another student said that he would be "a very different person" if he had had a different teacher. I felt very humble when I read this. That's the kind of teacher I want to be but I'm not there yet. I need to keep working at it.

So Mr Hankins gave me tools that I still use with my students today but I have adapted some of them so that every student can learn and grow, whatever their age, size, strength, flexibility or level of confidence.

I stayed with Mr Hankins until I completed my university studies earning a degree in the field of Electronic Technology but he gave me tools forty-one years ago that are still taught to my students to this day. Mr Hankins moved the School to Norfolk's 35th Street area in the early 1970s. It was conveniently situated just a few doors from the Mosque. He taught at that site until he retired. My first teacher was born on February 10, 1938 and passed away on July 17, 2011.

MY FIRST JOB

I was employed by a shipbuilding company as an electrician in 1971. It was the same company where I had spent the summers of '68, '69, and '70 working as an electrician's helper. I was on the night shift working on submarines. While working on the submarines, I met several guys who had martial art training, mostly Okinawan styles. One likeable guy introduced me to Sensei Pete Lukus, a US Air Force veteran who was working as a police detective and taught Shorinji Ryu twice a week at a ballet school. It was while I was training there that I learned how to use the stretch beams. I trained under Pete for nearly a year. I didn't think my seniors in that dojo were any match for me. Mr Hankins had taught me well. He was a bricklayer, so you can imagine what his hands looked like. Some of the students had strong hand techniques and were very fast, but my kicks oftentimes proved too much.

Eight months later, I was transferred to the Submarine Nuclear Design project (SND) to start my career in electrical design. It was about this time that Shihan (Frank Hargrove) returned from Okinawa Japan as a sixth Dan in Shorin-Ryu Karate, the youngest in the world at age twenty-nine. It was 1973. For a while, I maintained relationships with some of the martial artists I met while working in the yard and one of them told me about Shihan's return from Okinawa.

HANSHI FRANK HARGROVE

The man I have known and trained under for forty-two years and know today as 'Hanshi' was a 'Shihan' when I first met him. I was twenty-four years old, married and the father of two daughters, Davida and Patrice. I enrolled my oldest daughter into his classes. For me, I was not convinced that this guy had the agility to be any good. His dojo was an old, abandoned movie theatre on Kecoughtan Road in Hampton, Virginia. After several months of observing his classes and watching him destroy all comers with the greatest of ease, I became a believer. Training with Shihan involved a different type of discipline. The majority of the students training at Shihan's dojo were US Marines who were karate-trained in Okinawa, which meant that the training was very hard, very intense and very real. All classes, whether rain, sleet, snow or shine, began with a run to the beach and back, approximately four miles. This was at his dojo on Pembroke Avenue in Hampton. Then the workout: loads of push-ups, and sit-ups and mountain climbers. These were followed by blocking drills, which were sometimes static and sometimes with a partner. Then came Kata practice. Hanshi had accepted the rank I earned under Mr Hankins but it meant a lot of catch-up work. I had to learn all the Kihons, the Taikyokus, the Fukyus and the Naihanchis as well as all the associated bunkai and the Japanese terms.

Finally, Kumite (sparring). We did so much Kumite on a regular basis that wearing a groin cup was part of your Gi (uniform). You always had it on! In addition to learning the new Kata, I had to learn a new fighting approach. Whatever success I enjoyed while training at the previous dojo was short-lived at Shihan Hargrove's dojo. I have been a student training under Shihan's supervision for more than forty-two years from the age of twenty-five to my current age of sixty-seven.

Shihan asked if I had ever competed. I told him that I had. He asked how successful I had been. I said, "I have never won a thing." His reply was: "David, you have all the skill for being a winner! Who was your teacher?" I told him I had trained with Master Harold Hankins. Now, I don't know why I said 'Master Harold Hankins' because Mr Hankins really didn't have any martial art rank at all, he was a boxer and, whatever rank he acquired, it was through Master Kim. He was probably a first or second Dan, third at the most because black belts like those legendary martial artists Albert Cheeks, Mike Warren and Mitch Bobrow (who are now installed in Kukkiwon's Hall of Fame) were GM Kim's top students and Mr Hankins' seniors. Eventually, he reached 'Master' rank though.

Shihan went on to say, "Mr Hankins has taught you well, but no one has ever taught you how to win. This will be the only thing that I will ever teach you – I will teach you how to win because Mr Hankins has taught you everything else!" That's quite a flattering statement from a man who was sent back from Okinawa to unify Shorin Ryu and Okinawan karate in the Americas at the age of twenty-nine. Incredible: a sixth degree black belt in Okinawan Shorin Ryu karate by the time he was twenty-nine! No one had ever done it before, irrespective of nationality or ethnicity.

More often than not, Kumite ended in a bloodbath or a knockout session. Truly, you fought for survival in that dojo. Having good kicks was not enough to keep those marines off your butt. A hard quick kick in the head only encouraged them to attack more intensely. My jump-spinning back-kicks would only stop them in their tracks momentarily before they would charge again. You needed good, solid hand techniques too. It was both scary and fun and it was *real martial art*. Like Mr Hankins' dojo, the training sessions were two hours long but Shihan Hargrove's dojo was open six days a week. We were allowed to train every day! The 'squad' training sessions I have for my students today are nothing more than a replica of those early dojo days with those tenacious, determined and gifted fighters!

Coming from a Tang Soo Do background, I had sweet-looking kicks in comparison with the styleless, plain, 'get-the-job-done' Okinawan kicks. They were designed to put you in a grave, not to look pretty. I would discover many years later how superior Nakazato/Hargrove Shorin Ryu karate really was.

Shihan's classes were not always action-packed. On many occasions, he lectured on the finer components of karate-do. He explained the philosophical importance of waza and the attacking zone. We studied films as well! We always recorded each Kumite session and reviewed the footage. It was vital that we had a clear understanding of movement and positioning. This type of instruction was revolutionary for its time.

And win is what I did, not only in the ring; I became a winner in my day-to-day life. I became known as a tactician.

I learned how to take advantage of what my opponent gave me. If he lowered his hands, I attacked his head. If he raised the arms, I attacked his body. I conditioned my body so that I could take his best shot in order to deliver a vicious double-shot to his head and body. I learned how to manage space and positioning and how to predict my opponents' movements. I was not the most talented of Shihan's students but I learned how to simply outsmart them and confuse them with footwork and distance illusion. This is what Shihan taught me – how to win.

Most of the dojos which taught Goju Ryu, Shorinjiryu, Shorin Ryu and Isshinryu Ryu, all those hard-style types of Okinawan karate, were located outside the marine corps base. This was because they felt that the marines were easier to teach that hard stuff to, because they had been conditioned in their boot camps that way. Hanshi was in the air force and the others were marines, so first of all, even if I beat them, they would tell me how they had beaten me. I'd say, "What?" They didn't want to accept defeat. I beat the guy so that he can't even stand up, and he says, "Tell you what: try again, next time you might win." I might win?

That was the way they had been trained in boot camp and that was the attitude of spirit that they had. At the same time it was like a big family of brothers. Sometimes they didn't like one another, but you better leave them alone. No outsider could come in and interfere or say anything about them. We used to go dojo knocking. Dojo knocking is going to other schools and training with them for a night. It was interesting, especially when the people running the schools turned out not to be qualified to open schools and might not even be black belts.

Some of the karate-type movies that came on TV in those days sparked a lot of interest in martial arts but few people had formal training. I was given formal training but my friends were not. I bumped into one of my childhood friends many years later after he had finished his tour in the military. I was doing a ship check, and we got talking. He said, "We started off many years ago doing martial arts." We talked about the times when we tried to break plywood. My hand was swollen for about a month. I gave it all I could give it and I didn't know you couldn't break plywood. It was a piece of wood; I thought, "Just break this wood!" We tried to break two-by-fours and all kinds of stuff. Sometimes we would break it. I think it must have had a weak link or something, I don't know! That was what that was like then.

I asked Shihan the same thing I asked Mr Hankins. I asked him to teach me to be a teacher. At my request, all of my martial art teachers taught me not only martial art, but also how to be a teacher of martial art. Now! Did martial art resolve my anger? Yes it did, because as time went on there were many occasions when I avoided an altercation by apologizing to the person that I might possibly have offended. I did this just to make them go away. It didn't matter to me whether or not they thought I was a coward or that they were the better, the bigger or the stronger of the two of us. What mattered to me was that I had avoided a potential altercation.

This is the approach I still try to take today. I try to avoid anything that would trigger me into being potentially dangerous or harmful to someone else, even if it means that I walk away. That's the difference between how I was in my youth and how I am today as a result of the years of martial art training and the influence of my teachers. In my youth I would not have walked away, I would have fought. I don't know what my mentality was or why I felt that way, but that's the difference right to this day. I simply walk away unless I am cornered and I can't walk away. If I can't get out of the situation, someone is going to get blasted. It's as simple as that. I still have the explosive temper but I control it rather than letting it control me – that's the result of the discipline of martial arts.

I continued training with Hanshi after my wife left me but my daughter stopped. I just kept on training, training, it was very important to me. It kept my sanity through it all, and of course, I was a practising Buddhist by that time as well. I got caught up in that thought, the meditation. I bought into the whole 'martial package' from Asia, from the Japanese. I used to wear Kimonos and everything else. I wore Getas to class, the wooden shoes. I had wooden shoes! I ate a lot of rice and almost everything I ate, I ate with chopsticks. I hardly ate any American-style food. I had stir-fried rice and various types of teriyaki. I was basically living like a Japanese person in the United States. Because I was single, I had Japanese women always bringing me food: often Mondos, vegetable Mondos. They would always bring me stuff to eat at my house, so I was basically Japanese. Of course they knew I was studying Japanese martial art. I bought into the whole package of everything. Later I will discuss the ZEN influence that developed and shaped karate and the martial arts as tools for living, fighting and overcoming fear including the Five Minds – Shoshin, Zanshin, Mushin, Fudoshin and Senshin.

My new Japanese lifestyle disturbed my mother. I recall one time she visited my place. She thought that maybe I had been brainwashed, but I hadn't! I think that she later realized that I hadn't been brainwashed, but rather it was just something I had chosen to do. She would often tell her close friends that "her oldest son was trying to find himself." I don't really think that she ever forgave my wife for leaving. I did though! I never held it against her, because I knew from the bottom of my heart she never loved me. We married because it was the right thing to do back in those days. Sometimes the couple was able to survive the test of time and stay married for years – till death do we part – other times that wasn't the case.

Every Friday and Saturday night I would go clubbing. Disco was hot back then. I even took a battery of dance lessons at Fred Astaire Studio to learn proper ballroom dancing with a touch of disco added in. I got really good at it. I was quite popular with the old ladies at the Dance Studio and dancing with them led to me learning new steps before I was scheduled to. Life was kind of good, yet incomplete. I was without my girls – Davida and Patrice – but I had to make a new life for myself in order to be in a position to help them when the time came.

MY CAREER AS A DESIGN ENGINEER BEGINS

My career as a design engineer did not start until the designer strike of May 1975.

Although I had been employed as an electrical designer since 1972, I did not get the opportunity to design anything in my first job. Remember, I was colored and still living in the south. In fact, the state of Virginia was the Confederate Capital. I think that, philosophically, colors could never be put in a position or situation in which they could tell a white man what to do or offer direction or instruction. That was a 'no-no' in those days, and it meant that we did not get to perform higher levels of design.

In May 1975 the Designers Union went on strike for higher wages. The strike introduced me to 'contract design', where people with technical qualifications were hired by high-tech companies for a short period of time and paid an enormous amount of money. I had to continue working during the strike, so I found myself seeking employment through a headhunter, and a Union who gave my resume to the headhunter and a few of those contract firms. Most of the well-known contract firms were situated in the northern states. I was accepted!

By July of that year I was working in Huntsville, Alabama. Northern Alabama was a scientific community that didn't exist per se anywhere else in the United States. Huntsville even to this day is like that. It's where you have the Marshal Space Center. There's all kinds of sophisticated stuff there. Scientists from all over the world are in Huntsville and my first assignment was at the Marshall Space Center to work for IBM. It was very interesting work and I got to do real design for the first time. I made a name for myself in such a short time. My manager was very impressed and gave me more and more responsibilities. I was the only colored in the building apart from the janitor! The United States was still going through turbulent times and the word 'colored' was slowly being replaced with 'Afro-American' amongst the educated and social circles of learned men and women.

I never thought of the martial art as a hobby or a pastime. I always thought of it as medicine for me. It was not an option. I had to do this. I had to take my daily dose in order to stay healthy. One of the things that I loved probably equally as much as I loved the martial art was tennis. This was my pastime. In Huntsville I had access to acres of tennis complex, and I played tennis. They even had a section where you could actually play against yourself. So oftentimes I'd play against myself and the wall, pow, pow, pow. The wall was cut like the same dimensions of a tennis court. So I would practise. I would leave the office and go to the hotel, change my clothes, put my tennis outfit on, collect my rackets and I'd go and play tennis. I could play tennis on the days I didn't have a class.

I joined Master Chung's class. Although he was Korean he called himself Sensei Chung. I had a choice when I was looking around for schools between Master Chung and another instructor but I chose Master Chung who was in some Recreation Hall or something. Did he have a proper dojo? Maybe he did have a proper dojo but there was nothing fancy about it, nothing. I thoroughly enjoyed that.

The one thing Master Chung did not allow me to do was spar. I remember one night I was finally allowed to spar and I beat everybody in the school. Everyone was saying "Wait until Steve comes!" Steve was Master Chung's top student. I had beaten everybody else but Steve – he was away.

The night Steve came back, Master Chung told me to spar with him, and I succeeded in beating him as well. After the class in the dressing room Steve told everyone, including Master Chung: "One thing about Dave is, when you spar with him he just touches you, but you know he could have hit you harder." He said: "This guy has everything. He's so fast, you think you got him, you throw your technique, but he's not there! You just feel a pressure on your side and you look and there he is! You know that he could have torn your side out."

That was the type of fighter I was, so Hanshi had done a very good job of teaching me. That's why, no matter where I travelled after I left Huntsville, I always went back! Master Chung encouraged me to compete in the Alabama State Championship, which I did, winning first place in forms and second place in Kumite. I felt that I beat the first-placed winner but was awarded second place. My job lasted six months but I had earned more than a year's salary and gained loads of confidence in my design abilities as well as my martial arts skills.

I went back to Virginia and back to training with Shihan. My first day back in the dojo, I excitedly entered the school and greet Shihan by calling him Sensei. He responded immediately by telling me to drop and do one thousand push-ups. I remember him saying: "Do you call a dog a cat just because it got four legs and a tail?" He was furious because I had called him Sensei, but that was what Master Chung was called. All those months I'd been calling him "Sensei, Sensei," it just rolled off my tongue by accident. I apologized and explained how I had accidentally made the mistake, only after doing the push-ups. I was both embarrassed about my mistake and proud to be able to do a thousand push-ups in front of a client who had just signed up for classes.

I reported to the union hall on Monday morning to discover that the labor strike was still ongoing, so I accepted another contract assignment. This time it was deep south – Pascagoula, Mississippi. When I arrived there, I found lots of co-workers and designers from the first shipyard I had worked in. Finding someone to share an apartment with was a big challenge. No one wanted a black guy for a roommate. Luckily, two people I worked with on an old project, who happened to be from the north, proved to be the exceptions as they were more than willing to accommodate me. They had a three-bedroom apartment, making it ideal. They paid a price though! Many of the guys stopped talking to them. Lots of name-calling went on, but they were steadfast in their decision and we continued to stick together in everything.

So I went to train in Mississippi and I went to work building gunboats for the Shah of Iran. It's amazing: for the Gulf, the Persian Gulf. It was gunboats for the Persian Gulf, for the Shah of Iran! I did two projects for the Shah of Iran but that was the first one. In the office I did not get an overwhelming reception. I was different from the other blacks, I had a white girlfriend from France and I talked properly and dressed in a suit and tie every day. As it turned out, I worked directly for the Vice President of engineering. He liked my style. He had been a Naval Academy graduate and he was a real gentleman who loved soccer and coached a kids' league team.

My first task was to prepare a Heat Dissipation Report by compartment for the surface vessel that we were contracted to design and build for the Shah. Working directly for the engineering Vice President did not make me popular at all. In fact, their dislike for me increased, but I was untouchable which added even more fuel to the fire of their dislike. All but a few of the local guys kept their distance. I was too different. They saw me as a troublemaker from the north who wanted to change things and didn't know my place.

I developed an interest in Doberman Pinschers and was befriended by a local man who was impressed by my martial arts training, especially with fellow marines back at the dojo. He raised Dobermans from the Damasyn line of Dobermans, by Peggy Adamson. He was a mild-mannered man, very easy-going and down to earth. It was he who taught me about the Doberman breed of dog. He had studied the breed for more than two years before buying one. He decided on the Damasyn line, as they were big and bred for showing. The breeder was very selective about who she sold her dogs to. After a lengthy interview, she decided to sell my friend a puppy and he then waited for nearly a year before his dog arrived. Since he had no intention of showing the dog, he signed a contract stating that this was the case. His pup was six months old and had been neutered. A few months later, she sold him a second pup under the same conditions. They were absolutely beautiful!

This friend was a mechanical designer on the same project as me and another of the guys I met on this project introduced me to CB radio. Once I purchased my radio, I spent hours on end talking to every traveller that would talk to me. My handle was 'Peter Pan', the guy that taught the little folk how to fly. Being a progressive black male living in Mississippi and dating across the color line, I was left with very few, if any, options about how to spend my free time. There were people who would kill you over such matters in that part of the world, so I entertained myself on the CB radio every night. I looked forward to Fridays because the two guys I shared the apartment with and I would go out for dinner at a local restaurant. Boy did we turn some heads! One black guy and two whites sitting at a dinner table eating together. Virginia had its problems but Mississippi was another dimension! The social attitudes of the people were off the charts. Ignorant blacks were afraid of ignorant whites and this was my home for about fourteen months. During the week, we had an alternating duty roster, e.g. one would cook, another would wash dishes and the third person would take out the trash. After my chores, I was on the radio.

I was in search of a Doberman dog and was enchanted with the intelligence shown by another friend's Doberman, which was red and rust in coat colour. It was both voice- and hand-sign-trained and was able to do all sorts of tricks. It was amazing to watch as he worked. I would attend all the local and regional dog shows in my quest for a red-and-rust for myself.

While I was in Mississippi, my martial arts training suffered. One instructor seemed to take a dislike to me the first moment he laid eyes on me, he did not like me and would not allow me to take part in his class. He even objected to me watching. I'll never know why. I changed to another instructor but I didn't like him and he didn't like me. I told him who I had trained under. He must have known Shihan or known of him, so he didn't want someone like me in his class. I was just too skilled I guess. He could tell! Sometimes a good instructor can sense 'this guy will be a problem if I bring him in my class, he'll be a headache for me'.

After that I trained with another instructor who had greeted me with open arms. This school was all white but progressive in thought. Although this instructor liked and wanted me to be there to practise with his students in order to improve their skills, I didn't find it challenging. Having a place to practise on a regular basis was fine by me, but to be perfectly honest I didn't find anything demanding until I met Master Lee when I moved to Seattle.

I was in Mississippi until the judge kicked me out of there because of my driver's license. The situation in Mississippi was that you had to have your car registered with Mississippi license plates and a Mississippi driver's license within a week after moving there. I hadn't bothered to get properly licensed because I was on a temporary engineering assignment. Mississippi did not have an automatic system for checking vehicle licensing for Mississippi residents. The way they would catch drivers was by setting up a roadblock on a stretch of road where there were no turn-offs. They might do it Saturday afternoon or Sunday afternoon and they would catch people because Mississippi was sandwiched between two states. To the west it was Louisiana, and then to the east it was Alabama. Neither one of them had those requirements, nor did they have to pay personal property tax, which you had to pay for your vehicle in Mississippi.

People who were residents of Mississippi would actually purchase and register their cars in Alabama or Louisiana to avoid those taxes, so Mississippi had to catch them. It was a criminal offence and could result in a prison sentence. I had to go to court. It took a letter from the project engineer and the vice president to get me off without having to do jail time. The judge gave me two weeks or something like that to get it sorted out, and I decided that it was time for me to leave and get out of there and go back to Virginia.

It was a long drive back but I kept myself amused by chatting on the CB radio: "Breaker one nine, it's Peter Pan on the north bound side. What's your twenty (location)? What's it looking like over your donkey?" A truck driver would come back saying, "You got a clean shot back the other way, ok." I replied: "You got yourself a clean shot back to Mobile, ok. Thirty-three to ya. Have yourself a finnun (fine day), it be the Peter Pan gone!"

Thinking back now, my life was put on hold for fourteen months. Mississippi did nothing for my personal growth. However, I did experience a level of human hatred that has never been surpassed to date. On the positive side, on my long drive back to Virginia, I thought to myself that the few skills that I possessed had merit and were worth something to future employers.

I passed through parts of Alabama, Georgia, South Carolina and North Carolina. I was almost there. Mama and Daddy lived about thirty minutes from the North Carolina–Virginia border. I had plenty of time to think about what to do next. I knew the strike was still on. Some people had managed to find jobs elsewhere, and some like myself had had to leave the area to find work. Others made a career change. Still a few stayed on the picket line. Many broken homes occurred. The union strike had taken a painful toll on so many lives.

As for me, I did not know what awaited me. My relationship with my girlfriend had gone stale although I still believed that I had her heart and soul. I thought to myself, what next for me? What will I do? Thirty minutes more and I would be at Mama's house as I crossed the border into Virginia. The next thing I knew there was a loud siren and flashing red lights. I glanced into my rear-view mirror only to discover that a highway state police officer was directly behind me. I was not speeding. Why would he stop me? I pulled over to the shoulder of the road. The policeman followed me closely.

He got out of his cruiser and walked towards my car with his right hand on his revolver. He asked, "Driver's license and registration card, please". I immediately produced the requested items. After examining my paperwork, he asked, "Do you know why I stopped you?" I said, "Yes sir officer – my inspection sticker has expired."

He said "That's right." I began to explain that I was an engineer and had been on assignment in Mississippi for fourteen months and was just returning home. My destination was Suffolk, where my parents lived and where I would get the car inspected immediately once I arrived. One glance into my back seat told him that I was all packed up and on the move. A clothes rack was filled with suits and ties, and in the passenger seat sat my little red-and-rust Doberman Pinscher.

The officer gave me a nod and said, "Drive safely and have a nice day." I replied, "Thank you, officer." I took no chances. I drove directly to Mr West's auto garage to get my car inspected.

I phoned Mama to let her know I was in town and would be at her house as soon as the car was ready.

I had purchased Bon Maxwell the Red Niji from a backwoods, self-taught breeder of Dobermans while in Mississippi. He was Warlock–Kimbertal. The Warlock kennels were situated in Texas and the Kimbertal kennels were in Pennsylvania. I could not afford a Damasyn-line Doberman, nor would I meet the accommodation requirements that ownership of such a dog would necessitate. I didn't have a house to live in for myself, let alone for raising a pedigree dog. I had no girlfriend. But I had Niji, man's best friend, to keep me company. I stayed with Mama for a few weeks until I found a place in Hampton, a city on the peninsula neighboring with Newport News.

I visited my daughters on a regular basis but each visit left me saddened and lonely. They were living in an area of Hampton where I would never even have considered living. My former wife wanted a life filled with excitement and fun, while I wanted to distance myself from that lifestyle. Davida, the oldest, was nearly ten years old and Patrice was nearly six. They were both born in the month of November and four years apart in age. Losing the girls was the hardest part of the break-up. I wanted a storybook family with a storybook ending. I often described the girls as 'lotus flowers'. A lotus flower grows in a swamp. The more dismal the swamp, the more beautiful the flower. I thought that the housing complex they lived in was dismal.

One glance from a casual observer at the girls would prompt the question, "What are those two girls doing over here?" They were truly out of place. It was disturbing how helpless it made me feel. Each and every time I had the girls, I took them to the other side of town for treats. I needed them to know that there was another side, a better place, a different way of living. Many years later it has proven to have been a successful approach. My mother's residence would become an oasis for the girls once they reached their teens. Each and every Friday after school they would escape by catching a bus to Suffolk and spend the weekend with my mother.

My new apartment was actually a townhouse. It was very spacious, very stylish and conducive to living the life of a young professional. Pets were allowed, of course! I secured employment with a small company in Virginia Beach. My role there was an electrical aircraft designer. This company had won a contract to perform design support to Naval Air Rework Facility in Norfolk (NARF). This meant liaison almost daily with NARF to retrieve and/or deliver drawing packages. The work was okay, often challenging my poor mechanical drafting skills, but I persevered.

My manager was a lovely, likeable man from Minnesota in the mid-western United States. Nearly everyone in the office was from somewhere else, which meant the office staff was progressive in thought. The local people tended to be businesslike and were not inclined to be chatty. I didn't meet anyone there who shared any of my interests, but I enjoyed the variety of jobs that came across my desk. I was the acting supervisor. The salary was okay, although nowhere near my earning potential. Life was good. I had a respectable job and I visited my daughters on a regular basis and my girlfriend still kept in touch with me. I was able to continue my martial arts training at the dojo with Shihan and I had Niji, who waited patiently for me to come home.

I have not spoken very much about my Buddhist practice, which started in Hampton. I was a member of the Nichiren Shoshu Sokagaikai, a Buddhist sect based in Japan that chanted "Nam Myoho Renge Kyo" constantly but had five daily prayers that had to be performed. Now that I was back, I had resumed my practice. The faith was strongly practised in areas that had military bases or installations. Why? Because of GIs who had married Japanese brides. The Buddhist practice kept my mind from feeling sorry for my romantic state or rather the lack of it. I wanted a relationship with substance but did not meet anyone I thought could fill the void in my life.

I started back playing tennis regularly, at least two times a week. I even found a partner so I was able to play a few doubles matches. I played on the courts at Langley Air Force base and Hampton Institute, my favorite. When I was in college, Hampton Institute had been a rival college. They always had a strong tennis team. So now I was playing on courts where serious players played. Everything had fallen back into place, comfortable.

Just as things were settling down to a routine existence, I was summonsed to domestic court. It was centred on an increase in child support payments. My former wife had applied for state assistance. The first thing the system did was to evaluate the potential of the former husband to pay child support. The two of us had come to an informal arrangement that I should pay the bare minimum but that I would assist her in every way humanly possible, financially. This is what I did; after all, the girls were my children without a doubt. But once she entered the system, she lost control of the outcome. The court made what I felt were unreasonable demands.

When I openly expressed my displeasure about the decision,

the judge threatened to incarcerate me for up to twelve months so I shut my mouth. I left the courtroom after being warned about my child support payments. I remember crying all the way back to the townhouse and thinking, "The guy who encouraged her to leave me should be paying a portion. He's to blame. I did everything I could to make her happy. I was a good husband and father."

As I walked back to my house from domestic court, my mind was racing. It was stuck on thoughts and memories of some of my darkest days of early adulthood. I recalled how I had come home from the office on the 30th of September 1974, arriving at the usual time. I inserted the key into the lock and opened the door to an empty apartment; even the carpet on the living room floor had been removed. The only things left were two plates, two cups, two drinking glasses, two forks, two spoons, two knives, a bath towel and my bed, which came from Mama's house. That was it! I didn't have a clue where she had moved to or where my girls were.

I went to karate class that night and waited until Shihan (Hanshi now) and I were alone. I told him what had happened. He tried to console me and said that I would survive this situation.

When I reached my townhouse, Niji, my Doberman, was happy to see me, but I was not in the mood for playing. Once I had calmed down, I reached for the telephone and called my agent.

"This is Dave Harrell."

"Hi Dave, how can I help you?"

"I need to get the hell out of here right now!"

"Leave it with me and I will get back to you."

I got into my car and drove to the office with a sense of

hope and resolve. The next morning was a Tuesday and the agent phoned me at my office.

"How would you like to go to Tacoma, Washington?"

"Sounds great! When do I report?" was my reply.

"Monday morning, I'll send you all the paperwork to sign."

When I arrived home, I pulled out my atlas and searched endlessly for the Tacoma section in Washington DC. I phoned my tennis partner, who was a career veteran in the US Air Force, and asked him if he knew about Tacoma. "You fool, it's in Washington State, on the west coast," he said. "Pree (this was my nickname), you are going to love it. It's your lifestyle. You will fit right in. It rains a lot there though," he told me.

That night I broke the news to my girlfriend. She had mixed feelings about me leaving her again. She had reached the point where she wanted to renew her commitment to me, however the potential for racial problems blighted our relationship and I decided that the separation would do us both some good.

Moving would also mean that I would earn more money, which I desperately needed to do quickly to satisfy the courts. By Thursday I had received the paperwork and arranged for my agent to have a one-way airplane ticket to Seatac Airport in Seattle, Washington. But first things first! I had to tell my manager! His first reaction was to match the Tacoma offer but when he discovered what my salary would be, he asked if he could come along with me. The plan was that I should take six months' leave, satisfy the courts, and then return to my old job. This was the agreement. I flew on Northwestern Airline from Norfolk regional airport to Twin City Minneapolis/St Paul in Minnesota. From there, I flew to Seatac airport in Seattle. I arrived around 11:30am.

THE MOVE –
A FRESH START

I was met at the airport by Paul Duguid. I did not know Paul that well. We went out together a few times while in Pascagula. My agent had told me that Paul was in Tacoma and gave me his contact details. I phoned him and he was more than willing to meet me at the Seatac Airport.

Moving to Seattle was a big move for me. I was a long way from home, the other side of the country, four time zones from home. The people were very friendly. I saw very few blacks, an occasional one here and there. It was the first time I had been any place where blacks were not in the majority. In Seattle, jobs normally performed by black people were being done by white people. This was strange to me!

Paul and I collected my luggage at baggage claims and proceeded to his car. Paul was friendly and appeared to be happy to see me. We hadn't really known each other that well but I guess he was prepared to do his best to make me feel at ease and welcomed. As we travelled towards Tacoma on highway route 99, I was captured by all the sights of what would turn out to be my home for the next twenty years. Mount Rainier seemed to be the most dominant feature of the area. No matter which direction you travelled, it was always in view. We came upon an

Indian teepee, which prompted me to ask where we were. Paul replied that we were on the Puyallup Indian reservation. This was getting interesting. He informed me that he had to go back to work for a few hours but this would give me an opportunity to meet some of the guys I would be working with.

He told me that he had only been in Tacoma for three months, and that he and some of the Pascagula gang had come directly to Tacoma when that job had come to an end. We arrived at the so-called shipyard. Was I in for a surprise! The shipyard where I had previously worked had taken up five miles of waterfront with shipways and dry docks, fabrication buildings, office buildings, thirteen piers and an apprentice school. It also had a gymnasium and an athletic football field with a track. The shipyard in Pascagula was a mini, scaled-down version of the first one, but the site of my new employment in Tacoma was just a spot on the water!

We entered the engineering office, and I was greeted by some of the Newport News–Pascagula bunch. One guy walked up and greeted me with a handshake and a smile. I asked myself, "What in the hell is going on here? I am being accepted right away." Paul introduced me to the electrical design team. The team was divided into sections: Interior Communication (IC), Power and Lighting, Propulsion Plant, Electronics and Cableways. Monday morning would be my start date and I was assigned to the Cableways group with two other guys.

The pay rate was great – twelve dollars and fifty cents an hour. In addition, we were paid one hundred and ten dollars a week living allowance, and all hours over eight were paid at the rate of time and a half. With a minimum of twenty overtime hours each week, I was going to earn nine hundred and eighty-five dollars a week or nearly four thousand dollars a month. Prior to the strike, I was making six dollars and twenty-five cents an hour at Newport News Shipyard. And the strike was still on. The minimum wage back then was two dollars and sixty-five cents. I was earning less than four dollars above minimum wages.

There was obviously some resentment of contract designers amongst those designers who worked directly for a company. My relationship with these people was strained from the beginning.

Paul had been asked to become a deacon of a church. He had preconceived ideas about what an official of the church should be and did not feel it was the right thing for him. His wife did feel that he was worthy to hold a stately position in the church however, so taking design assignments away from home allowed him to delay the process.

Paul allowed me to stay with him in his one-bedroom apartment. I slept on the davenport and lived out of my suitcase for three weeks. Paul was not the neatest of people in my eyes (though I confess that I can be over-zealous when it comes to cleaning). In fact he was somewhat disorganized where house-keeping was concerned. I would get the chance to give it a good cleaning though with surprising results. Paul had met a native North American from Vancouver, BC while visiting the King Tut (Tutankhamun) exhibition that was touring North America. They had become good friends and alternated weekend visits. It was Paul's turn to visit Vancouver. He left straight from the office that Friday and would not return until late Sunday night or early Monday morning. I had plenty of time to give the house a good scrubbing. When I had finished, the apartment was shining. I just knew Paul would be pleased! Besides, I felt guilty for not paying him for staying. I received my first cheque that very Friday.

Paul returned around 10:30pm on Sunday night. He walked into the apartment, looked around from room to room and became enraged at what I had done to his house. He demanded that I find somewhere else to stay by tomorrow. I was puzzled by his reaction. I guess I hadn't understood that I could cause offence by my actions and that I should not interfere, particularly since I was a guest. I used my lunchtime to visit and make a deposit on a one-bedroom apartment within walking distance from the office. After work, Paul helped me transport my belongings to my new apartment. We than went to the waterbed warehouse and I purchased my first waterbed. I arranged to have it delivered and installed the following morning. On Monday night I slept on the floor of what would be home for three years.

Paul arrived every morning around 8:15am to give me a lift to work. By the time we arrived, the office was full and all present had settled in for the task at hand. The other two members of our group would often come in shortly after us. Most of the designers started working at 5am or 6am which allowed them to leave around 4:30pm or 5:30pm, having worked ten to twelve hours. Remember, all hours worked in excess of the core eight were paid at the rate of time and a half. A few of the others were night people. They preferred working late into the evening. I was an early morning person and wanted to be at my desk before 6am so I needed to find another mode of transportation that would allow me to do this. After work finished the following Friday, I went to the local sporting goods shop and purchased a twelve-speed bike and started riding to and from work on it. My starting time was 5:30am. Paul picked me up on rainy days.

Paul's expertise was in equipment arrangement. It was his job to decide where all the electrical and electronic equipment was to be placed throughout the vessel. The rest of us had the task of routing the wiring to those pieces of equipment throughout the vessel. Designing and developing the installation methods were also our responsibility. That was an enormous task!

With all the ventilation ducting and piping to also be routed, constant negotiation with the mechanical and structural groups was required in order to establish routine envelopes for each discipline on the vessel. The job was fun yet demanding. And everyone got along together.

I wondered if they had had a change of heart about racial matters when they observed how harmoniously people of all backgrounds interacted in Washington. It was certainly an eye-opener for me. In the early days of my move, I thought I was dreaming. What a contrast it was to some of the other places I had lived and worked.

Huntsville had become a city built from the ground up by the aerospace industry. Most of the engineers and scientists were from somewhere else. That meant they brought with them a sensible approach to living and interacting. Personal skills were more important than skin color. Oh, but if you dared to venture beyond the city limits, it wouldn't take you long to find the opposite. Most towns had pockets of daylight where companies had brought in engineers from other parts to work for them. These people brought their preference for racial harmony and equality with them.

Washington State was different. The locals had a natural liking for all people. In many ways it was still the last frontier. If you were to drive in any direction, within five minutes you would be out in a rural area. I liked my job and I worked very hard at it. My assignment was the engine room and everything below main deck, fore and aft. It was the biggest career challenge of my life. There was cable wiring that started in the pilot house, travelled down into the engine room, and ended by aft in the steering gear room. This meant creating cableway envelopes on both the port and starboard sides of the ship. Some cables required separation to avoid signal interference so a dedicated cableway had to be established for them; and the cable volume was massive.

I worked undisturbed for months. One Sunday morning, my Lead came over to my desk to look at my design. He hit the roof! He became very upset saying that my design was all wrong – and I had over-designed areas. He said that, first thing on Monday morning, he was going to get rid of me. I did not know what I was doing wrong. He crushed my drawing up into a ball and threw it into the trash can. He left the office after that and I retrieved the drawing from the trash can, unfolded it, and put it in a safe place.

First thing on Monday morning, the Lead was in my manager's office complaining about me and suggesting that I be dismissed. When he finally left the office his face was beetroot red. I was called in by my manager and told that my Lead was not pleased with my work, but that everyone deserves a second chance. He said he was going to put me to work with Jack who was responsible for power distribution and lighting.

I didn't know much about Jack, he was pretty quiet. He spoke with a deep southern accent so I had my doubts. Jack, though, was a contractor like me and he was great to work with. He and I worked as a real team. We defended and looked out for each other as well. I didn't know much about power and lighting at first but I learned real fast and became better at designing systems than Jack. Jack and his Lead also clashed occasionally over the interpretation of ship's design specifications. Most of the time, though, Jack would lose the argument.

The Iranian Patrol Boat Project progressed on steadily. More and more designers from every discipline were recruited for the seven-boat build. We lost a few too. Some left the project to work elsewhere but were quickly replaced. One of these replacements was Rob.

While at Newport News, I had been selected to work on the new Trident Submarine prototype project. We had completed eighty-five percent of the design on an at-risk budget when the Federal Government decided to give the project to EB in Groton. Our engineering efforts were bundled up and transferred to EB. The Federal Government awarded us with the 688 Los Angeles class submarines. Years later, Tom Clancy would write a book about them, *The Hunt for Red October*.

Rob was a damn good designer! He was very quiet and sometimes reluctant to answer questions. Jack and I got our input directly from the propulsion plant design. We were responsible for generating the power distribution system for Rob's output. Interfacing with Rob was a daily routine.

Months later, on a Sunday afternoon, while my manager was checking the engine room cableway drawings, I whipped out my original design to compare it with what my Lead (the one who rejected my work) had designed. It was almost identical! My Manager said, "Well, I'll be damned!" The plan had backfired and the Lead had lost credibility. He had not established enough of a space envelope in the early part of the project and now he was catching hell to create new space for the required cable volume. The expression on my manager's face said it all. I could see that he was glad that he had made the right decision about keeping me on.

Like Jack, my manager had served in the navy for more than twenty years. He used to say, "There's the right job for everyone. As a manager I've got to find it and make the person feel comfortable doing it."

Each time I moved to another engineering assignment, I consistently did two things. Firstly, I would look in the yellow pages of the phone book and look up the address and phone number of the nearest Nichiren Shoshu Buddhist temple. Then I would do the same for the nearest karate or martial arts school. Moving to Seattle/Tacoma was no different. The Myoshinji Temple was located in downtown Seattle. And there was a Tacoma Chiku (branch house) as well. The practice here was very laid back and the rhythm was slow compared to the Virginia/DC area. The whole south-eastern seaboard is the heart of the Bible Belt, so any religious practice other than mainstream was taboo. It was a real challenge to get people to attend a discussion meeting. The moment you said Buddha you were speaking to deaf ears!

On the other hand, the west coast was different in that people were not afraid to know or explore, so the area lacked resistance to the unusual or the strange. I would regularly attend meetings but I just couldn't connect. Slowly my strict practice was reduced to my one-bedroom apartment.

When he had heard where I was going to be working, Hanshi had said, "Okay, when you get there I want you to train under Teruo Chinen, he teaches Goju Ryu." I said, "Yes sir." I later found out through Steve Armstrong that Chinen was over in Spokane, Washington, which is eastern Washington, a six-hour drive away. The drive was freeway all the way but still, a six-hour drive. So I couldn't study under Chinen. He said, "Okay, then study under Steve Armstrong."

Steve Armstrong taught Isshin Ryu which is an Okinawan karate as well. I didn't like Isshin Ryu so I contemplated studying under Jerry Gould who was Shorin Ryu, but was one of Shimabuku's students. I rejected that idea, however, and decided that it would be a good time to expand my martial arts knowledge and learn something different. I went back to Hanshi and said, "I'm going to learn stick fighting." He said, "Okay." So I joined a class and started learning Kenjutsu. I was also studying Kendo. I'd been studying Kendo for a number of years under Jeff Marsten, until Master Lee, and I was studying Tai Chi Chung – Wing Chung-style Tai Chi Chung, under Sifu Joe Clark, who has since died. I had run out of options regarding karate training, so I simply trained and practised at home. I had lots of room. My apartment had only two pieces of furniture – a waterbed and a game table in the kitchenette with two metal folding chairs. The living room was bare.

I biked to and from work and walked to a restaurant for dinner every night. It was only two blocks from the apartment. The apartment complex was situated behind the athletic field of the high school. It had a tennis practice wall that I sometimes used on weekends. I had loads of time alone to think and think about everything. I thought about what to do with my life. It occurred to me that this was an opportunity for a fresh start. It was a chance to become a brand new me and to have a new identity. How did I want to be thought of and who did I want to become? That's what I had to decide. Even my style of dress had to change, I thought, but to what, to whaaaaat?

Six months passed by quickly but I was not ready to go back to Virginia. I had told my boss there, as well as my girlfriend, that six months was all I needed to sort things out, but I really liked this Pacific Northwest life, although I couldn't tell you why. I couldn't express it in words until one Friday night at the hottest disco in town. I was seated at the bar where I would have dinner and then, by default, be in the lounge before the crowd gathered. Two well-dressed girls were seated beside me. One had just returned from the washroom. She said excitedly, "He's here, he's here!" The other girl quizzed her about what he looked like. She said, "He's sitting next to the door with a white dress shirt, brown cuffed trousers and a pair of Baileys." (Baileys were expensive designer shoes.)

The girl next to me was so excited about this cat being here that I had to find out for myself who he was! Their excitement had me excited, so I drifted out into the lobby and headed for the men's room. On my way, I scanned the area on the lookout for boy wonderful. I spotted him. The girl's description was very accurate, and he was the only black guy in the lobby! As I strolled back to my seat at the bar, I was confused. Something was missing from this picture. As my butt touched the bar stool, it hit me like a ton of bricks. The one thing that this white girl sitting next to me did not say was "He's the black guy with the… " She was color-blind. As I thought deeper, I realized that this whole area was color-blind. Since I arrived, I had experienced something for the first time in my life: I was accepted for who I was, not what or who I looked like. It would be easy to establish a new identity now, a new me, and it felt wonderful!

Fall was about to set in and it became apparent that I needed a car. Jack was a collector of old Saabs, 96 series, so I bought one from him, for seven hundred dollars, I believe. The Saab was the first front-wheel drive vehicle I had ever owned. It was light blue and looked like an upside-down bathtub with tyres. It had a standard shift transmission and an optional floating clutch. It was basic transportation that got me where I wanted to go and that was all that I needed. Even though I was totally independent of Paul now, I was very grateful for his kindness and often invited him over for a steak cooked over the barbie. His favorite cut of meat was the porterhouse and he liked it medium-well. To ensure the steaks were tender, I would marinate them all day in my special brand of spices and seasoning. You didn't need teeth, they would melt in your mouth. They were often served with mashed potatoes and corn on the cob.

Paul was the first baseman on our company's slow-pitch softball team. He was a big target for the infielders stand at six feet four or five. But his vision was so poor that once you threw the ball to him, it was a hope and a prayer that he would catch it. I played a variety of positions but mostly the outfield. With my foot speed, I could comfortably chase down a fly ball and catch on the run, not bad for someone who had been so clumsy as a kid. We had a game at least twice a week, one during the week, and one on Saturday. There was always a cookout after the games. It was fun. A relief after the stress of the long hours we all worked.

Of course, it was not all equality and harmony! One person

would regularly make a gesture of a monkey holding onto a tree branch and turning loose. Then he would say, "Don't let go." Paul would be furious but he never said a word to me about it. It didn't happen to me though! The word was out that I was a martial artist. Besides, I was congenial to all, but was never what you would call over-friendly. Those indifferent guys walked softly around me.

About a month after I arrived in the Pacific Northwest, Paul took me to Vancouver, BC. It was the first time that I had left the United States. It was exciting, going to another country. I wondered if they spoke English. I was so stupid and naive in a lot of things. I had lived a sheltered life back in Virginia. My brothers and I were provided with whatever we wanted, most of the time without even asking. It was simply there to have. Now, I was on my own and had to learn to make decisions on my own. I had never even bought myself a shirt or a pair of trousers or suit. It had always been taken care of by my parents and grandparents.

We entered British Columbia at the Blaine Washington crossing. Blaine was a very simple border town that came to life at weekends when the Canadians would cross the border to get their cars filled up with petroleum. The petroleum cost in Canada was double the price. Even when you considered the currency exchange rate, it was still cheaper for Canadians to travel to Blaine for petroleum. We crossed the border on the Canadian side without any interrogation. Paul told me that it depended on who was on duty. There were some real jerks on duty at times.

Vancouver was just another big city but the people were lovely, very friendly and polite. We checked into the Four Seasons hotel, a five-star hotel located in the heart of downtown

Vancouver. We had a light snack in the coffee shop, then we headed back to the room to freshen up and to change into our suits and ties. We then set off down to the basement of the hotel where the hottest disco in the city, Annabelle's, awaited us. The queue seemed to be endless. When we found the end of it, we took our places. We started chatting with the two girls directly in front of us. Then I thought, "We are hotel guests, that's got to mean something." I walked to the front of the line and approached the bouncers. I told them we were hotel guests and asked if we had to wait in the long queue. The bouncer said, "Absolutely not, show me your room key." I reached into my jacket packet and produced our room key. The bouncer said, "You are in." I told him I had to get my friend and our dates. He said that was fine. I walked back to Paul and signalled to the two girls and we all strolled inside. The place was jumping with all the latest disco tunes. We had a dancing night that I will never forget.

We woke up to a sunny Vancouver morning. We hurried for breakfast and afterwards started to explore the city. Paul took me straight to Stanley Park. At the entrance to the park was a bunch of people who looked to be Chinese who were practicing Tai Chi. They all moved harmoniously together, at the same speed. They were smooth and graceful, meditation in motion, I thought to myself. We stood and watched the movement for a while. The whole scene reminded me of how much I missed my karate training. "I must find a school where I can continue my training," I said to myself.

The park had everything – trails, beaches, an observatory and a full-scale zoo. It even had an amusement area for the little ones. There were joggers and cyclists and people on horses. This was a one-stop spot. Cafes, restaurants and boathouses lined the waterfront. There were even waterskiers, and canoes of all sizes cruising along the lake. We spent the entire day there. It was an action-packed day. At about five o'clock, we arrived back at the hotel, exhausted. I had to have a rest because Annabelle's was on my mind and I wanted to be fresh and ready for another evening of dancing.

We knew the routine now so we entered Annabelle's without a hitch, and danced the night away. My dance lessons at Fred Astaire Studios were paying off. I was heavily sought after by a lot of the girls who were good dancers. I had a ball! Paul did too, even though he wasn't a disco dancer. On Sunday morning, the hotel featured a lovely brunch buffet. Every fruit and pastry you could think of was available: waffles, pancakes; you could have your eggs cooked a thousand ways. Paul had a Denver Omelette – diced ham, cheese, tomatoes, onions and green peppers. I settled for an omelette with onions, green peppers, black olives, a few jalapeños and a hint of cheddar cheese.

Then it was time for the thirty-minute drive from downtown Vancouver to the USA border. The pleasant drive back to Tacoma was interrupted by the immigration officer. I think I had drifted off to sleep for a moment. "What's your citizenship? Where have you been? How long were you away? Where do you live? Bring anything back? Have a nice day!" It was a drill that I would go through each and every time I entered the USA. Sometimes more intense interrogation was applied. Sometimes the whole car was searched. The interrogation was often done in a tone of "How dare you leave this country?" A tone I thought sounded contemptuous. Notwithstanding, we arrived back at my apartment in Fife around six o'clock. The journey had taken us about three and a half hours. We had made good time as there was very little road traffic. I grabbed my suitcase from the trunk of the car. We exchanged goodbyes and Paul headed to his place, only fifteen minutes away.

It seemed to me that each and every Monday produced more people. We got a new guy called Phil who was tall, blue eyed and fair haired. He was a swimmer and had an athletic build, but was a quiet and reserved person. The usual Monday morning was filled with the same stuff. I got right into it. I was doing cableway layout drawings that required constant inter-discipline interfacing. Penetrating structured bulkhead required program approval and you had to make double sure that no one else occupied the space on the other side. There were times when the cableways resembled a roller coaster zigzagging and weaving between ventilation ducting and hydraulic piping. You had to spend hours on end negotiating for space before you could draw a single line. This process continued day in and day out, from Monday through Sunday, with the occasional weekend off.

Weekends were spent in Vancouver. We bounced between Annabelle's and Sugar Daddy's, and met some of the same people at both. I became very good friends with a guy called Van and started going out on Wednesday and Friday nights and sometimes Saturday too. I taught him how to disco dance in my apartment after work. I would ride the bike and he would drive ahead in his hatchback. He became very good with the moves, turns, spins and tucks but his beat and rhythm was slightly off.

Our first trial was on a Wednesday night at Ye Old Ram in Tacoma, directly across the street from Tacoma Community College. It was a tavern students' hangout with a mall disco floor. It served as a perfect place to practise. He did well but his timing was still a little off. Van always displayed more confidence in dancing while his skill at being smooth in movement was left behind. The real test would be at HT Hotspurs on a Friday night, where the serious dancers congregated, and on a Saturday at the Doubletree. Weeks later, Phil, who claimed to be a hot disco dancer, decided to hang with us one Friday night at HT Hotspurs. This blond-haired guy learned two lessons that night.

The first lesson was: he wasn't that hot on the dance floor! The second lesson was that being blond, blue eyed and white meant nothing in the Pacific Northwest. At our table sat one black, one white and one Asian, all looking around for a potential dance partner. Van spotted a red-haired beauty staring in our direction. Phil said arrogantly, "She's mine, fellows," and was off to her table in a flash. Van and I also left our table in pursuit of dance partners. I found a partner quickly and the two of us danced about three or four songs before we both decided to take a break. I returned to our table, arriving about the same time as Van. We both had big smiles on our faces. We found Phil sitting there like a bump on a log. I said, "My partner was pretty good," and Van added, "Mine too!" I asked Phil how he had gotten on with his partner. He said, "She said no!"

Van glanced in the direction of her table and said, "She's still looking over here," Van said confidently, "My turn!" He removed his glasses and strolled over to the redhead's table. Phil and I got up and cruised around looking for another dance. After a few numbers had played, I returned to our table to find both Phil and Van chatting. I ordered another Coke while asking Van at the same time if she had been a good dancer. He replied, "I don't know. She said no!" In the same breath, he said, "She's still looking over here." But I dared not look in her direction.

We talked casually for a couple of tunes so that I could get my breath, then I said, "My turn." Walking to her table seemed to take three or four minutes as I prepared myself for the embarrassing NO! I asked, "Would you like to dance"? She replied, "I thought you would never ask!" She was a very good dancer. She was tall and long legged and prettily built. Her height made her perfect for me with the spins, twists, turns and tucks. We danced until we were both out of breath, even dancing to the slow songs to catch a second wind. Dancing slowly gave us a chance to talk, she said.

She admitted that she had spotted me on the dance floor at another club the week before. She thought that I interpreted the music the same way she did and had a strong desire to dance with me. She added, "I've noticed that you are very popular with all the girls who are good dancers." She continued talking, "When I spotted you walk in with your two friends, I said to myself: 'I'm going to get a dance with him tonight'." I said, "I'm Dave." When I walked her back to her table, I noticed that there were two girls sitting there. They were friends of hers. I joined them for a moment and she introduced them, before I returned to Phil and Van. I said, "Her name is Emily and she is an excellent dancer." Van was talkative as usual but Phil was noticeably quiet. Eventually, we all sat together at one table, the six of us, but Emily only danced with me that night.

The next morning we were all back at work, where Van's desk was directly behind mine, so we could comfortably work and talk. Phil was situated some distance away. Phil drifted over to my desk and sat on the drawing table stool. He began to speak as if someone had drained him of all his energy. He said, "I never thought there would come a time when I would have to compete with a black guy for a white girl." I reminded him that he was no longer in the south. I told him that I had also had to make mental adjustments since moving to the northwest. He asked if Emily had gone to my place and my reply was "Yes." He said, "Wow!" After that, he was fine and our relationship grew.

The three of us were inseparable. Wednesday, Friday and Saturday was our weekly disco routine. I met Sarah, and Phil met Jane at HT Hotspurs on a Friday night. Sarah was a happy faced, east European-looking girl: a long-haired brunette with big brown eyes. In fact, her hair reached her waist. I had actually seen her at the Ram club several nights earlier but had not noticed her dancing. I had recalled an incident while driving home where a car pulled up beside me and someone honked the horn, getting my attention. I noticed someone's butt protruding from the rear passenger's window of the car. I thought it was a sick joke and drove off, never giving it another thought.

Sarah later shared with me that it was her butt, sending me a 'moon' out of anger because I hadn't danced with her. Sarah had a spirited craziness about her. She was a very determined young lady.

Jane was quite a bit like Phil – quiet and shy but bright. Though good friends, it was obvious that the two girls had come from different backgrounds. The five of us had good times when we were out together – Van being the odd man out. Van was a good Catholic who believed strongly in abstaining. He had one word to describe our behavior: terrible! One of my favorite singers was Ann Murray, a Canadian country and western singer whose songs had hit the pop charts as well. Her songs were ideal for slow romantic dances with someone special towards the end of the night.

GRAND MASTER LEE

In 1982, I noticed that a Taekwondo school had just opened up, so I told my wife (I married a Canadian named Carole on April 9, 1981). She said, "You know you miss that!" I said, "Yes, the Tai Chi for health is okay but I need a structured class, I miss the structured classes." In a typical Tai Chi class there were maybe fifty guys in the room and everyone was practising on their own. Everyone was doing something different. I didn't like training this way. To me it was just discord. I preferred something a little more unified and structured.

I met and talked to Grand Master Lee who was a seventh Dan. I asked him if he would accept me as a student. He said that he would and he brought me in as a blue belt. Initially I thought "Of course he isn't going to allow someone new to come in with a black belt from another instructor." How wrong I was about GM Lee!

He was a gentleman! He was only concerned about my growth as both a martial artist and being a good person. I started out as a blue belt and in less than a year's time I was a black belt in Taekwondo with Master Lee. He was like a second father to me and raised me as if I were one of his sons. I was family.

He gave himself to us. The workouts were equally as hard and demanding as those led by Mr Hankins or Hanshi Hargrove. There was a twist to his approach though.

If he shouted at you, "Your kicking is wrong!" or "Same time you kicking same time your leg back," in his roughly spoken English, you never doubted his genuine concern for your personal improvement. You never thought for one moment that he was angry with you. Simply put, he wanted you to want to do the techniques correctly. After all, the martial art has been systematically passed down from father to son, master to student for decades.

In Scotland, I have found that it is hard for some people to get to grips with the idea that I shout because I care, not because I am angry. Remember that the kihap (yell) initially makes them uncomfortable! Perhaps they don't often encounter a teacher who really cares about them and their sense of well-being and self-esteem, not about winning medals. Perhaps they are not used to teachers being passionate about what they are teaching and wanting to be sure that they are remaining true to their own teachers. Most of them 'get it' eventually though! Maybe when they feel that inner warmth, excitement and sense of satisfaction that comes when they have finally mastered a technique. After that, they just keep on growing.

GM Lee did not only orchestrate those challenging workouts, he performed them with you: punch for punch, kick for kick, block for block, push-up for push-up, sit-up for sit-up, Poomsae for Poomsae, kihap (yell) for kihap. He was the leader but he was also one of us! You can make students do what you want them to do by standing at the front giving instructions but to make them want to do it, you have to show that you are willing to do it with them. This is how I teach my students and how I insist that my assistant instructors train with them.

When class was over, the black Gi that GM Lee wore was soaking wet with sweat. And so were our doboks.

GM Lee suffered with hayfever, so when entering the dojang, if you observed him sniffing or with a tissue in hand, you knew his hayfever had flared up. This as an early warning sign that tonight's class was going to be even more demanding than usual.

Friday night class was a treat! More often than not, the adult class attendance was low. The reason for this was that most families would dine out on Friday night. So GM Lee often gave those present special techniques or additional information to show appreciation of the sacrifices that these students made to attend class. He was always willing to give a piece of himself to his students. We often hear about the importance of a leader 'walking the talk' as a means of inspiring followers. GM Lee did that and he inspired me to want to be like him. I also have classes on a Friday night. Some students never attend these classes as they are otherwise occupied, but a number of students attend faithfully every Friday. Following in GM Lee's footsteps, I try to give these students something extra to show that I understand and appreciate the fact that they have forfeited other activities that their friends are enjoying in order to come to class and learn. Some students are shown special techniques that they can make their own if they go away and practise them. I know that these students will practise because they want to learn and to be the best that they can be.

For GM Lee, it was never about money. It was about passing on the martial art message to the next generation. That would one day be his gift to society. He gave it to me and now I am trying to give that gift to you.

Of course, now that I was doing Taekwondo training again, I also resumed fighting in tournaments. I had been going to tournaments because Jerry Gould knew I was Hanshi's student

(Hanshi was a Shihan at that time). I would go to visit him and to his dojo from time to time and he would say, "Look, I'm having a championship so at least come to it and watch." I would go to all his karate tournaments, so I knew all the karate guys and all the karate guys knew me, but I was looked upon as the karate guy who did Taekwondo, the Korean style. It was okay, it didn't bother me.

I also went to Vancouver and got involved with the karate guys up there but because of the large Chinese influence, Kempo, a Chinese style of karate, was kind of strong. Kempo had been introduced there by Ed Parker's influence. It was okay.

I developed myself a little reputation of being a person of knowledge. I never did any karate fighting on the West Coast but I did Taekwondo with Master Lee. It was good doing the Taekwondo thing but I was always getting in trouble for punching guys in the face. I was used to karate and in karate you were able to punch in the face. I had to really tone down and focus on punching to the body, punching to the body, punching to the body. Never getting any points for that but I would hammer the chest cavity so hard, sometimes they would want to actually disqualify me because I was punching so hard. I would punch to set up for my kicks you see, but nevertheless I did all right.

Beginning as an instructor with Master Lee really happened by accident. The marine industry had started going by the late 1970s/mid 1980s. The marine industry was dying so he was about to lose his job. The only way he was able to save his job was by going on night shift.

By that time I had earned third Dan so I was actually teaching his classes for him while he worked at night. It was good. That's how I got into the role of teaching Taekwondo, by teaching Master

Lee's students for him. My teaching skills had already begun to be developed from working as a Sempai and as a black belt for Hanshi for all those years. Karate and Taekwondo are different disciplines, however, and I had forgotten pretty much all of my Kata because I was really trying to make this Taekwondo a goal since Taekwondo was up-and-coming. It was exhilarating – the flashy kicks, the high kicks! The breaking was more exciting than Kata, Kumite, Waza, Bunkai, or so I thought! That's how I got caught up in it. It led me to Master Lee and the Taekwondo thing and developing a relationship there.

Because I was developing my teaching skills and the students were doing very well, Grand Master Lee said, "Okay David, we have new championships, you have to take the students to the championships and you have to act as if you are me," which meant that I had to be rubbing elbows with all the Korean Masters. It was easy to say but hard to do because they knew I wasn't Master rank and they didn't want anyone around who was not Master rank. Nevertheless Master Lee at that time was president of the Korean Masters Association so they accepted and respected his decision to have me deputize for him. So there I was amongst the mix of them, being respected as and treated like a Master Instructor, which I wasn't, only because I was acting on behalf of my instructor. Many people regard Taekwondo as a sport, but it is a martial art and Grand Master Lee was a martial artist. Nonetheless, the students did very well in the championships they took part in and I became a Taekwondo Instructor.

I have kept in touch with Grand Master Lee over the years and often describe him to my students. I sometimes think that my students must know nearly as much about my teachers as I do. I want them to have that connection though. It's important to have roots to provide the nutrients and water from the soil. Without these, a tree will not grow and without strong roots a martial artist will not flourish. So, I am proud of my roots and faithful to them, and I want my students to be proud and faithful too. In my last conversation with Grand Master Lee a few days ago, he told me that he was proud of me. This brought tears to my eyes. That such a thoughtful, talented and generous man and martial artist should be proud of me made me feel both humble and excited. It spurs me on to greater efforts. That's what a great teacher does!

LEAVING TEACHERS

I didn't leave Mr Hankins, I simply finished university and I was employed in a different city. I told Mr Hankins that, since I was going to be living in Hampton, I thought I should study under Shihan Hargrove (Hanshi) and he told me that was a very, very good choice. He said that there was no doubt that this man had a knowledge of the martial art that was second to nobody in the Americas.

In fact, I can recall when my daughter, my first-born, Davida, tested for her green belt, Mr Hankins actually came over and watched the grading. I recall when Hanshi put the green belt around Davida's waist, she must have been about eight years old; her feet were bleeding from running barefoot for seven miles. This was an eight-year-old running seven miles barefooted on the pavement! In the winter! In the month of November! He looked at me with tears in his eyes. He said, "David, you should be proud of that little girl." I'll never forget that. Her little feet were bleeding. She wasn't crying but her feet were bleeding. They were numb from the cold. That's how hard a teacher Hanshi was. He didn't teach gender martial art; Mr Hankins didn't teach gender martial art and I do not teach gender martial art. If you were in his class, he taught you martial art, full stop. You could be anything you wanted to be, he taught you martial art, and Hanshi was the same way. And so did Master Lee.

My training under Hanshi was accepted and approved by Mr Hankins, so I've never left my teacher. That's why all of my teachers are still alive, except for Mr Hankins, who died a few years back, the result of diabetes. Master Kim died fifteen or sixteen years ago, if not longer. He's been gone a long, long time. I'm not quite sure how he died. I don't know. All of my other teachers are still alive to this day and I'm still in contact with them, on a regular basis. So I have never left a teacher. I just went from one teacher to another with the other teacher's blessing.

The best teacher I've ever had was Hanshi, there's not a shadow of a doubt. If one were to ask me what I learned from each one of them, I would say that Mr Hankins taught me not to fear. He instilled in all of us, 'I do not fear you', and I think primarily because he was a Muslim. Muslims are taught to fear only God. So he taught me, 'Have no fear', especially when fighting. I didn't have that anyway though, so it made it very, very easy for me.

Hanshi taught me how to win, not only win in an altercation, but also win in life: how to be successful at getting things done.

What Grand Master Lee taught me though is priceless! He taught me how to love, how to really care and be concerned. It was important that you knew certain things about him. He was unlike all the other teachers, whose personal life, personality and person, were private. You didn't know their birthdays, sometimes you didn't even know where in the hell they lived. They just lived somewhere over there.

Grand Master Lee was open. You knew his birthday. He wanted you to know that. He wanted you to know certain things about him. I think that can be the missing link for a lot of today's martial art instructors. They just teach and there's no cohesive relationship between the student and the teacher. So Grand Master Lee taught me how to love my students.

Grand Master Duk Gun Kwon taught me the business sense of martial art. He taught me how to do it in such a fashion that, not only do you preserve the integrity of the art, but you also learn how to make money from it. It is sometimes very difficult to combine these two, however. Quality can get lost. I know of some instructors, for example, who have a belt grading whenever they need money for a car or a down payment on something. Some may insist that students have more than one or two uniforms, or that the students need to change their equipment. These are all types of tactics to get more money from them. That's basically compromising the integrity of the art. I don't do it that way. There are other ways of being able to do it and make it rewarding for the students. So Master Kwon taught me the business sense that most martial art instructors don't have. They can teach you skills but they don't know how to make money from what they teach you in an honest fashion. Master Kwon also taught me the value of the 'seminar' approach to training. He arranged seminars, which I would fly down to and attend (it was at one of these seminars that he awarded me my sixth Dan). Since moving to Scotland I have held my own training seminars, which my students have told me they find challenging and rewarding. Master Kwon still advises me to this day and I am grateful for his continued interest and support.

All my instructors have played very important roles that changed my life and are still changing my life, even to this day.

They have certainly helped me to build constructive, productive relationships. I don't experience jealousy if a student wants to open their own school. I want them to open up a school. Unfortunately, maybe because I want them to have that, I don't have any students that have schools. They all still stay with me, under my direct instruction.

I think also, because of what I teach, they're afraid that if they went out somewhere, they would miss the teaching, which basically suggests that they don't feel they have the knowledge base to teach yet. I guess this is good, in a sense. It's flattering if a student who has been with you ten, twelve or even fifteen years still thinks that there are things that you can teach them. I've been with Hanshi for forty-two years and every time I get a chance to go home and visit Dad, I'm in his dojo, training or being critiqued, or teaching his students. What a privilege and an honor!

PART TWO
TEACHING

TEACHING MARTIAL ARTS

I opened my first dojang on October 13, 1991. For the very first time, I felt alone, unprotected, without supervision, no one to follow, no one to blame.

This was when I started developing my own teaching style. Having moments of doubt and uncertainty, I was forced to trust in my training for the first time. For the very first time, I had to take the lead. I was the teacher, the mentor, t'e leader.

Success from my dojang opening advertisement campaign came in the form of seven new students on the first day and six or seven more in the following days. None had any prior martial arts training, yet I was scared to death. I was actually shaking! My new students stood in front of me in lines and rows eagerly waiting for me to give them their first lesson.

I asked myself: what am I going to teach them?

Where do I start?

Ahhhhh!

Running, stretching and calisthenics is where I got control of my moment of fear and began to take command of my class. This was the routine I repeated with them for about a week before advancing to the start of teaching basic blocking and kicking. I found that the students loved the hard workout.

Those hard warm-ups became the prelude to all of the lessons to be taught in each and every class. By the end of each session the floor would be soaking wet and the walls would be weeping with sweat.

I led each session by example, just as Grand Master Lee had always done. I performed all that was asked of my students along with them, count for count, block for block, kick for kick and punch for punch. The fitness level at the Institute was second to no martial arts school in the area.

Our tournament record was a testimonial to this fact. When we went to tournaments, the question was not whether we would win any first places but how many first places would we win?

We became known as the 'House of Sweat'.

I will share with you a true story.

It was my usual habit to run every morning, whatever the weather. One winter's morning, I found fresh snow. Inspired by tales from Grand Master Lee about what his training had been like in South Korea, I decided to run barefooted.

One of my students witnessed this scene while en route to High School. A few days later, my students proposed that we should have a school song and offered to share one that they had written. The song went like this:

"Saw an old man running down the street.

Had no hair on his head, no shoes on his feet.

Said, hey old man where you going to?

Traditional Taekwondo Institute.

Say old man, now ain't you too old?

Better leave that stuff to the young and the bold.

Sonny, sonny don't you be no fool.

I'm the Chief Instructor at the Taekwon School!"

This song, written by my students in Seattle, is today sung by my students in Scotland.

The very first fixtures that were installed in this first dojang were mirrors on the walls. The same was true for my second dojang. Every dojo and every dojang that I have trained in had mirrors. I practised my blocks in front of a mirror. I practiced my Kata and Poomsae in front of mirrors. I practiced my kicks in front of mirrors. That all changed when I moved to Aberdeen, Scotland, with my wife, Nicky and my baby son, Isaiah. I no longer had the luxury of having a store-front site. I was reduced to a recreation hall for seniors and a church. The only fixtures that the dojang had were the puzzle floor mats that I brought over from Seattle, a few free-standing heavy bags and some handheld kicking paddles. I have had to learn how to teach without mirrors and I had to develop ways of teaching things that had not been required to be taught in the States. When I moved to Scotland, I noticed two things straight away: students did not yell and their footwork skills were terrible. Their movement and rhythm left a lot to be desired. Why? Because they did not dance as a general rule.

It is very rare for a student with a natural sense of rhythm and timing to join my program so I have introduced music as a teaching aid to help students develop their rhythm and timing. The music is also a tool for communicating with the students and I have a selection of music carefully chosen to influence pace, mood and motivation as well as movement skills. This is also why I have games with the 'Little Tigers' where they can step, slide, run, hop, skip and jump or chase a ball, activities that children indulge in much less than they did in my day. The Xbox and the television have had a profound effect on the activity levels of young people of today!

Now the 'yell' was a real challenge and remains a challenge

for nine out of ten students who join my program. Some Scots think of Americans as 'loud' and 'pushy', and value the quiet, reserved approach to the world that allows people to push past them in a queue, or makes them apologize when someone has bumped into them. Encouraging young children to yell is less problematic than persuading adults to do the same. The running and jumping and kicking as well as the noise made by their peers soon has the children joining in the fun. On a more serious note, I do emphasize to children (as well as adults) that the voice can be a weapon. It can discourage aggressors and bring rapid help if in a threatening situation.

Now the adult students have more difficulty with the yell! When I explain that it is a tool that needs to be developed, as well as the fact that it is a systematic method of breathing, they understand these facts. Nonetheless, getting them to put it into practice is still very difficult. Even though the person next to them is yelling as loud as they can, the new student is still inhibited and reluctant to do something so unnatural. I then have to try a different approach. When do you get the best out of people? When they are tired! When they are drawing on the last of their innermost strength! So when someone doesn't yell I make the class do push-ups or sit-ups or mountain climbers, or all three. They are exhausted and frustrated and, at last, their inhibitions disappear. Maybe they are screaming at me. It doesn't matter. They have learned how to yell and they have learned that it is a positive thing.

Unbeknownst to them I am also working on a second goal. I am strengthening their bodies as well as their minds. I make the male students do the push-ups on their knuckles and everyone has to do push-ups on their hands as well as their fingertips.

Their *fingertips* not *fingerprints*. This strengthens different parts of the hand and I can convey the concept of the hand as a weapon more easily and help them to relate this concept to the techniques they are performing when they practise Poomsae.

As I have already mentioned, teaching without mirrors was another challenge for me. How to get the student to perform a technique correctly when they cannot actually see how it looks? First of all, I obviously have to demonstrate the technique several times. Next I give a clear and detailed description of what is happening, explaining what the attacker is doing and how the student needs to perform the required technique effectively to defend him/herself. I demonstrate to the students what can happen when the technique is performed incorrectly. This allows the student to create a mental image of the scenario and the correct execution of the technique. This visualization trains the body to perform the skill.

This approach is very successful for the more commonly used techniques like the basic blocks, e.g. Lower, Middle Inside, Middle Outside and Upper Blocks that are present in most of the Palgwe and Taeguek Poomsaes.

However, for the blocking and/or striking combination techniques that are uniquely different and appear much less commonly in those Poomsaes, I find that the most useful teaching approach, that guarantees success, is to identify and dissect these blocking and/or striking combination techniques. Once I have done this, I then create movement drills that students practise in order to become familiar and comfortable with these combinations of techniques. This process takes place just before the students have reached the stage of learning the actual Poomsae.

For example: Drill Number 1

This drill focuses on one unique movement in Poomsae Taegeuk Sa Jang (number four):

Sonnal Momtong Makki (knife hand body block), shown in *Illustration 1*.

Ill. 1   *Ill. 1A*   *Ill. 1B*   *Ill. 1C*

Drill Number 2:

Also targets one specific unique movement, which is the fifth movement, Jebipoom Mok Chigi (open hand face block accompanied with a knife hand strike), shown in *Illustration 2*.

Ill. 2   *Ill. 2A*   *Ill. 2B*

Drill Number 3

From Palgwe Chil Jang – four uncommonly used movements were selected.

1. Arae Hechyo Makki (low wedge block)
2. Apchigi (front kick)
3. An Palmok Hechyo Makki (palm inward body level wedge block),
4. Eotgeoreo Eolgool Makki (high X block)

Illustration 3 shows this drill in action.

Ill. 3   *Ill. 3A*   *Ill. 3B*   *Ill. 3C*

Drill Number 4:

Again from Palgwe Chil Jang I selected another three sequential movements.

1. Momtong Yeop Makki (inside-to-outside body block)
2. Eolgool Baro Chireugi (reverse punch to the face)
3. Immediately followed by an Eolgool Makki (face block)

Ill. 4   *Ill. 4A*   *Ill. 4B*

Illustration 4.

It is worth noting that, in *Illustration 1*, the follow-up counter technique is a Sonkeut Chireugi (spear hand thrust strike). From a sports competitive point of view, the execution of this technique in the Poomsae is only required to meet artistic standards and to be symmetrically aesthetic. This applies to all counter-attack striking instruments, whether with the knuckles of the fist, the blade of the hand or the tips of the fingers. The actual martial applications of counter-attack striking instruments that appear throughout all Poomsae, whether Palgwe or Taeguek, require further developmental considerations, for example, performing push-ups on the fingertips (not fingerprints), push-ups on the knuckles of the fist and blades of the hand. At the Institute, all students are encouraged to practise these conditioning exercises as well as striking the makiwara (striking board). Practicing these conditioning exercises will lead to martial fit counter-attack striking instruments. The martial mindset is also conditioned to support the counter-attack striking instrument applications.

The next consideration has to be how to make these drills

meaningful to students so that they do not simply become rituals. I do this by introducing students to the idea of a training partner. Throughout my training I have always had a partner. Sometimes my partner is the student who has been allocated to me by the instructor. Oftentimes though, my partner is an imaginary partner. Even though he is imaginary, I know what he looks like and how big he is. I also know his name. Whenever I perform a technique, he is there and I can see whether or not my technique has been successful. I can see if he flinches in pain, if he drops his hands, if he stumbles or if he smiles because I have not hurt him. I see this and I know what I need to do next! All of my students have been encouraged to have an imaginary partner and I have asked each of them to tell me the name of this partner! When they practise their Poomsae I can see if their imaginary partner is with them or if they haven't brought him with them to this particular class!

To a certain degree, all I know is martial art! As far back as I can remember, I've been doing it. I can recall at class night in my senior year in high school, we put on a type of play for our parents and whoever wanted to come in to watch us. The only role that they'd found for me involved me walking onto the stage wearing a pair of boxing shorts and boxing gloves, to demonstrate my ability to defend myself to some underclass man who was puny and skinny and looked emaciated. That was the only thing that they thought I could do, that was how I was viewed: as somebody who was pugnacious. That was it. It's unfortunate but that was the picture that I painted.

I can kind of relate to Einstein a bit. Only a bit, because I'm not an Einstein! I can relate to him in the sense that I don't think I was ever expected to achieve much compared to the other people in my high school class. There were some very, very bright people in that class of 1967 and nearly the majority of them flunked out their first year of university because they chose to go to some of these top-rate universities.

When they went off to these universities, they got their butts spanked because they were competing against kids who surely had much higher academic skills than they had. I did show academic promise but the first thing I think about when I think of the David of my youth is the David who gets into a fight with somebody, because someone did something to him. That was the David J. Harrell that everyone knew. Even though they recognized that there was academic potential, when they thought of me, they thought of fighting, not academics.

That's why I liken myself to Einstein, because Einstein was not ever expected to achieve very much. He didn't fit into the mould that teachers – especially the secondary school teachers – have a tendency to want to place kids in. It's a structured environment that has the expectation that everyone should comply with that particular environment. Anyone who doesn't meet those predetermined expectations is considered an underachiever. I guess that's how I look at myself.

I don't even know how in the hell I was able to achieve the successes I have had in my career. I have obtained highly paid jobs whilst some of my classmates achieved significantly less. I have succeeded in attracting talented students who have become successful in many walks of life and who credit my martial art training with having been a positive influence on their lives. What was so special about me? What did I do? What did I say? How did I merit the accomplishments that I've experienced and enjoyed? What did I give to my students that motivated and encouraged them? It's really hard to pinpoint anything specific. I guess I just have to say what I am.

Asking me how I teach my students is a bit like asking Michael Jordan how does he do the things he does. I watched a series on the Public Broadcasting Service (PBS) about jazz. They seemed to have categorized jazz artists as being the most skilful of musicians. Every night at a performance they had another opportunity to perfect their skill. That meant that no performance was ever duplicated. This is how I treat my martial art training and in fact, almost everything that I do. It's almost like each time I get the chance to do it, it's another opportunity to get it right. There's no rehearsal for that. That's the thing: how do you rehearse something that is dynamic? That's live?

A good example of what I mean is my belt grading on April 27, 2013. That was an excellent grading! To get those people to do what they did again would be impossible. They showed up and performed. The best that they could do, if asked to do it again, would be to try and improve what they personally felt like they had underperformed in. Just that alone would suggest that it is impossible to duplicate that which they did. It goes without saying then, when I see those students in their next class, I'm seeing a different student from the one I saw last week. I'm seeing a different student who feels a little bit differently about him or herself, who feels a little more confident in his or her skills than they did last week. Now I've got a clean canvas to draw a picture on.

That's what makes it so challenging, because what I see is what they're going to get. That's only for a period of time, because again, it's dynamic. Whatever I teach you, at some point, it's going to be in contradiction to something new that I teach you. It's in contradiction because what worked then, won't work now, because we're neither one of us at the same point that we were. It's always on a fresh starting point, a new starting point. A new opportunity! A new chance! I teach what I am able to see can be achieved by the student in front of me.

I think having a vision and foresight – and being encouraged to think in that fashion – about looking for another tomorrow, was induced in me from the womb. In fact, my entire generation was chosen as the generation that was going to change things. It happened in the wombs of our mothers, who wanted a better day. We were taught to see the possibility. Maybe that's what triggers my God-given ability to see things, to understand things and to perceive things. I always want something better. I wanted to improve the situation, the circumstances; after that, anything and everything is possible.

Martin Luther King did a brilliant job of saying, "I have a dream." All of us from that generation had a dream, and it wasn't that clear to us what that dream was, but we knew that we were all on a mission of some sort. Today, my program is made up of people from all walks of life, all ethnicities – a variety of ethnicities I should say – religious backgrounds – I mean, it's just everybody is there, everyone's represented. Except that my audience is not black; it's made up of white people and people who, in American society, would be considered white. I think that's one of the things that really leaves me baffled; that here's this black man that came out of the arms of segregation who has won the love and respect of whites. In doing this I think I have lived up to the expectations of my parents even though the expectations that my parents levied on me, and the 'allowed' expectations that society would accept from me, were two different things.

I can recall in the first grade, I always wanted to be an engineer. I didn't know what in the hell an engineer was, I don't even know where the notion in my head came from, but I always wanted to be an engineer. I remember my teacher asking everyone who they'd like – or what they'd like – to be. I said, "An engineer." The very first parent–teacher conference they had, the teacher said, "We have a problem with David. We need to talk to him, because David, he's talking about being an engineer." I remember how my mum blessed that teacher out (that's a saying we have in the black community for chewing someone out). She was angry that a schoolteacher would discourage someone from being the best that they could be. My schoolteacher was only looking at it from the point of view of the segregation situation and not having the vision to think that possibly things might change.

When Phil was leaving Tacoma to take a job in San Francisco he said, "David, you are everything that my mum and father said you weren't, and now I've got to go back and tell them that they were wrong." He needed several drinks before he managed to say this to me. There are two things there. One, he was able to identify that there was something uniquely different about me that contradicted his parents' teachings; and two, it was so significant that he found it necessary to go back and tell them. That's something else.

That's where I am, and I truly don't see color. I may make reference to it, so that people can understand where I'm coming from, but I don't see it. I just see opportunities and

I see potential. I see those that are capable of being successful and contributing to society, and that's what it's all about. You know, leading a life that puts a mark on some spot that says, "I was here and this is what I did." It's apparent that I've been given the opportunity to be just that. All praise be to God. What a blessing.

Since becoming a Muslim, I discovered that, in Islam, there are three things that you can take with you to the grave. The first thing is giving someone knowledge that they can use long after you are gone. That's truly a blessing. The second thing is asking God for forgiveness and acceptance of your deceased loved ones, relatives and friends, praying for them and their salvation while they're in their grave. The third thing is building a mosque. You can't take the wealth you may have accumulated to the grave, nor your fame. I've been blessed with something that I can give people that will outlive me, possibly for several generations. It's certainly the case for my instructor's instructor's instructor.

Would Chibana Sensei ever have dreamt that his martial art, Shorin-Ryu Karate, from the tiny island of Okinawa, would one day be taught and cover every spot on the globe?

There is documented evidence of Chibana's knowledge of Kata and techniques taught to him by Ankoh Itosu, who himself was an accomplished martial arts teacher. Chibana Sensei's ability to teach the martial art was an art within itself, reflecting the lengthy apprenticeship he had with his teacher, Itosu. This progeny overlapped into other Okinawan-based karate styles as many instructors of those styles visited Chibana's dojo regularly.

I just finished calling Hanshi, to ask him, how did he teach me to be a teacher? This is based on the fact that most of my students consider me to be a very good teacher. I don't know where that came from, except for the fact that I was taught to teach, but I don't know how I was taught to teach.

To reiterate, and to reinforce the concept of my relationship with my teachers, I just actually phoned Shihan, who's now a Hanshi (a ninth Dan). I asked him; I said, "Would you kindly tell me how you taught me to teach? Because I don't know, but you know." The principle thing is that most of my teachers are still alive, and I still have a day-to-day working rapport with them, and this is what I'm trying to pass on to my students; that the relationship between us should be like a mother–father or father–son, father–daughter, whatever it is. It's not just something that goes and comes because you get angry, you find someone else to go to. You work it out, and you remember that person, who is in your life, wants to give you things and give you tools to help you in your life, not to harm you. Unfortunately, some of the things that he may tell you to do or not to do, you may take offence at because you enjoy doing them. You think that it's okay. But they have the wisdom and the foresight to see that maybe that's not good for you. It may be good for other people but it's not good for you. Rather than ask Hanshi, I should have been able to answer my own question. What he and my other teachers have conveyed to me over the years, through words, but mainly through actions, is that it is this relationship – respect and caring and willingness to give and share – that makes a good teacher, not technical skill or knowledge. This is why I have never left any of my teachers.

EVERYONE IS NOT THE SAME

It was March 28, 2015 at my 261st Keup belt grading since moving to Scotland seventeen years earlier that it was brought to my consciousness what I already knew. Some very small number of parents believed that rank promotion consideration should be granted to the athletically gifted as a top priority. Typically belt gradings serve as an indicator of a student's level of progression and development. Obviously, some students develop sooner than others and are capable of displaying skills normally taught at an advanced level. A parent expressed an opinion that those who had higher levels of skills should be allowed to advance at a faster rate than other students. The examiner, however has to look at the bigger picture. Being able to display techniques does not mean that a student understands the movement or its application in a variety of settings. One of the tools used in determining the student's comprehension is the essay that is submitted as part of the grading process. The manner in which the student presents that essay shows whether or not their comprehension of the martial art and the application of techniques equals their ability to simply display a technique.

Every individual in the dojang is unique in every way. No matter how much instruction is given nor training hours spent in the dojang, some of my students are only going to reach a skill level category of 'fair', while others can become 'good' with very little effort. The student who is every instructor's dream is the one who has sound personal discipline, is willing to train consistently, and has good athleticism. This student can become great!

My teaching methods and training processes have been developed with the aim of ensuring that each student is educated in a way that encourages them to reach their individual best. This is where I have always devoted my efforts.

As it has consistently turned out, it is those students in the 'fair' and 'good' categories who have become some of my most productive and successful. Why? Because they have to work very hard to achieve a satisfactory performance level. They work from the 'gut level' and are, more often than not, self-starters. They require very little motivation, just direction. Another of their attributes is that they are usually very observant and very aware of finer details of following instructions given. They are the first to ask questions or seek clarification in matters of body mechanics and basic motion.

MY RELATIONSHIP
WITH KUKKIWON

To a certain degree, all I know is martial art! As far back as I can remember, I've been doing it and I have visited South Korea many times. My first visit was in October 2000. Two months later, I would become a Muslim.

No matter where you travel in South Korea, it's always the same: their emotions are kept hidden and their faces are inscrutable. I have never felt unsafe in South Korea yet I know I could never live there because I believe you must be Korean to enjoy living there. Outsiders have difficulty fitting into the culture.

Unfortunately this means that you can feel like an uninvited stranger, not a guest. The South Koreans have a thirst to succeed in every area on the global stage, yet remain cautious of developing familiarity.

I visit South Korea several times a year. I want to teach my students the very best so I believe I need to stay connected to the birthplace of Taekwondo. Of course there are exceptions to the general rule and I have met some loving South Koreans. Warmth and friendship are always wonderful treasures to discover.

Since my initial visit to Seoul, I have visited 'The Morning Calm' (South Korea) more than twenty times. The most recent visits were as a guest speaker at the 2012, 2013 and 2014 Leaders' Forums. The honor of being invited to speak on more than one occasion is something that I will treasure forever. These visits gave me and my teaching style global exposure and actually led to me deciding to write this book, which I started in my hotel room on December 25, 2012 while in Sharjah, United Arab Emirates.

It was at the 2014 Masters Instructor Course, held at Muju Taekwondowon, when Master Norbert Amefu from Ghana said to me, after an open discussion lecture about martial arts history: "GM Harrell, you could have taught that class to us. With your knowledge you should write a book."

I replied: "I started writing one a year and a half ago."

He said: "Well, let me know when you finish it! I'll be the first to buy your book."

Master Amefu had been the fifth martial arts master to tell me that. I promised Master Amefu I would make a serious effort to complete the book by the end of 2015, God willing.

THE HEART OF
THE MATTER

So far, I have given you the background information about those events, professional adventures and life experiences that led to the formation of who I am. I have explained about my training and conditioning and satisfying my apprenticeship requirement as a martial artist. Now that the reader has a complete picture of my personal profile, I would like to get to the heart of the matter:

What I see through my teaching eye and how I respond to what I see!

Instructors who have limited teaching tools tend to use them inappropriately and indiscriminately, the 'one size fits all' approach. Each individual is unique, however, and has his/her specific needs, preferences, strengths and weaknesses. This creates multiple tasks for the instructor for which multiple tools are required.

With this in mind, I think we first need to explore learning styles. After all, teaching styles and teaching approaches must be adjusted to suit the learning style of the student, if desired results are to be achieved.

Case in point – I offered a recreational Martial Art for Fitness program at a local health club. When the program initially started, its members included students who had black belts in Shotokan karate and students who had no prior martial art training. This program was designed to incorporate select karate techniques such as blocking, punching and kicking into a 'high intensity' workout.

The black belters had not formally trained in a number of years, so I decided to start with basic techniques. They welcomed practising basic techniques.

These basic techniques, however, were actually very advanced basic techniques. I quickly noticed that the novices in the class were having difficulties learning the body mechanics of movement. Moving the left arm in one direction while moving the right arm in another direction, with a step to the front or to the side, was a major challenge for the novices. Some had even begun to show signs of frustration and bewilderment.

Teaching experience told me that I had to adjust my teaching style, but how to adjust it was unclear. I first had to identify the learning style of the student.

Now for the technical stuff!

Some of you may be wondering what I mean when I talk about learning styles. Others will be thinking that having an understanding of learning styles is unnecessary for martial art instructors, as it is up to the instructor to decide what to teach and it is up to the student to learn, or not! If this is what you think then you are mistaken. Our dojangs and dojos are diverse student communities, each one with his or her unique learning style and learning preferences. It is the instructor's responsibility to determine what is best for his/her students and adjust instructional methods and approaches to suit. A mismatch between learning styles and instructional style can be disastrous!

I have always been of the opinion that, if the student fails, it's the instructor who is to blame.

Everyone has learning style preferences, some students favor visual learning, some prefer auditory learning and yet others learn by doing (kinesthetic learning). As instructors / teachers, it's our job to take the time to assess the needs of every new student and that assessment should include the learning style that they prefer. Teaching is like fishing... you need to use different lures for different fish, and you need to use different methods for different learners. We need to think about and plan to use a variety of instructional methods so that, at some point during the class, the instructional method matches the learning preference of the individual student. If we do this, the student will work harder to learn during those times where the instructional method is not a match. Obviously this is only one of the factors you need to consider when you are choosing the instructional approach you will take for a specific lesson. Other factors to be taken into account include:

The intended specific outcome or purpose (if you want to teach students to perform a low block correctly, they will need to perform the technique)

Size of group (learning by doing can be difficult if you have a large group and few helpers to supervise)

The content sometimes dictates the method (for example, teaching students about the history of their martial art will necessitate more of a 'talk and chalk' approach.

As far as the novices in the health club were concerned, I quickly discovered that I needed to break techniques down into their component parts and demonstrate each part individually, before putting it all together. I also found one student in particular had a strong preference for auditory learning so every demonstration had to be underpinned by detailed explanations. This student, who had been becoming frustrated and discouraged, has progressed into one of my most dedicated, enthusiastic students.

THE IMPORTANCE OF ESTABLISHING SOUND FUNDAMENTALS

Establishing sound fundamental martial basics is extremely important irrespective of the students' athleticism. One of the biggest mistakes the instructor can make is not putting enough emphasis on basics, whether it be blocking or striking (with hand or foot).

This understanding came to me during moments of reflection on my Mugairyu Iaido training while in Tokyo, Japan.

Sunday morning around ten o'clock, the Go Dans, Roku Dans and Nana Dans (fifth, sixth and seventh degree black-belters) would stride into the dojo. Without a word, they would start to practise. Each and every time these high-rankers came into the dojo, they began their practice by performing all the basic sword manipulations (draw drills and cutting drills) repeatedly, before starting their Kata. They would not advance to the next drill until they were completely satisfied with their execution. Slowly, methodically, all the basic drills were completed to a level that satisfied the individual. Only when he/she had achieved personal satisfaction with his/her performance of each drill, did the practitioner move to higher-level skills practice. When they started practising their Kata, everyone followed the same disciplined procedure.

To give you an understanding of the magnitude of this austerity, there are four draw drills, eight basic cut drills and twenty Kata – ten from a seated position, five from a standing position, and five running. These have all been learned before reaching second Dan black belt, but not perfected. The same approach was taken to each drill or Kata – only when the person had performed to their own satisfaction and their own exacting standards would he/she permit themselves to progress. This was what these high-ranking sword men and women would perform before the advanced Kata were practised, one after the other, with the same mindset. They knew the importance of mastering the basics. Their skills were nothing short of excellent! Without conversation, totally focused on the task at hand. The Grand Master, Niina Gosoke, would appear around noon to begin the weekly training sessions.

Thus, having a firm understanding of movement mechanics is vital to ensure good martial art technical execution as the student advances up the belt-ranking ladder.

Another basic tool that often goes underdeveloped – the eyes.

One of the most powerful, humbling, devastating and debilitating tools in a martial artist's arsenal is their eyes!

With just a slight turn of the head, accompanied by an icy stare in their direction, a hustler or an aggressor is sent a silent message saying 'take your ugliness elsewhere, it will not be tolerated'.

A soft, intent look can send a signal to all parties involved in an emotion filled discussion to calm down.

Eyes that gleam with enthusiasm and pleasure give hope to the weary and confidence to those being challenged at a belt grading.

Yes! The eyes are tools too, one of those tools being a weapon. Just think of how your mother was able to get you to correct your behavior with just a stare, or to give her approval with an enthusiastic look.

So, at the Institute, teaching a new student the importance of looking straight ahead, in the direction of movement, is part of his or her basic training and they are routinely reminded. With time, the student becomes armed with the ability to use his/her eyes to convey a variety of messages in a range of situations.

Another sense that should be developed in the student is his or her hearing and presence awareness. A technique I sometimes use to assist this development is to blindfold a student so that he or she has to rely on their hearing and surrounding awareness.

STANCES

Let's take as an example simple punching drills while in a 'Horse Riding Stance'. There are many lessons to be learned from this simple yet very important basic drill. The student learns:

Fig. 1   *Fig. 1a*

Horse Riding Stance (Figs. 1 & 1a)

- Posture:
    1. Head / body positioning
    2. Hand positioning
    3. Body weight positioning
- Hand–eye coordination
- Eye movement control
- Balance
- Leg strength

- Recoil mechanics
- Hand speed
- How to develop focus

Each one of these items listed is a lesson in itself. If any one of these components, as I would like to refer to them, were to go undeveloped, chances are the student's overall skill performance would be adversely affected. Not to mention the effectiveness of the student's martial art technique execution.

Let me explain this in more detail, one component at a time.

1. POSTURE:

- Head/Body positioning – hold your head upright and square with your shoulders. Your feet must be pointed frontward and shoulder-width apart. Bend knees in a 'horse riding' fashion. Keep your spine straight. Rotate your pelvis upward and keep your shoulders relaxed.
- Hand positioning – at the start, position both hands at your sides at the same height with the palms up. Next, fully extend your left arm out towards your front centre while gently rotating the left hand to palm down (See Fig. 1). Retract the left arm back to your left side, palm up again. Now fully extending your right arm toward your front centre while gently rotating the right hand to palm down (See Fig. 1a). Repeat these movements ten times, alternating from left to right. At first start slowly, then gradually increase your speed. Now try this alternating hand movement with a clenched fist.

- Body weight positioning – keep both feet flat on the floor with your weight equally distributed on both legs. You should feel all four corners of each foot (See Figs. 1 or 1a).

2. HAND–EYE COORDINATION – the target in space should be your front centreline, so your hands or clenched fists should aim for that point with your eyes looking straight ahead at a projected eye level. You will be able to see your hands moving out in front without moving your head.

3. EYE MOVEMENT CONTROL – learning to look straight ahead in space will strengthen your eye muscles thus widening your peripheral vision. In other words you will be developing wide-angle vision, which will allow you to see more without any head movement.

4. BALANCE.

5. LEG STRENGTH.

6. RECOIL MECHANICS – so the alternating 'hand positions' repetition will soon become second nature along with the desired hand displacement relative to the side of the body. It is sometimes referred to as 'chambering'. Nearly every Poomsae or Kata requires chambering. Being cognizant of its importance in your early stages of martial development will become an invaluable tool for gradings and competition performances.

7. HAND SPEED – with the left arm fully extended and the right fist clenched in a chamber position, you are ready to punch. The speed of your punches depends on the speed of your chamber-exchange mechanics. Imagine pulling your extended left fist back to the left side chamber position as fast as you can while extending your right

fist, in the right-side chamber position, equally as fast. The speed of mass in space gives you *power*! So the faster the recoil mechanics, the faster the hand speed, the more powerful the punch.

8. HOW TO DEVELOP FOCUS – at the very early stages of your martial arts training, try to pretend you are working with an imaginary partner who has exactly the same physical properties as yourself. You are then targeting your punches, blocks, kicks and strikes at this partner. Sometimes aiming for the face and sometimes the body. This partner will help you to focus or direct your attention. With your imaginary partner you are less likely to look from side to side or around the room. Rather, you will keep your focus.

In September 2015, I submitted a research paper to the Kukkiwon Research Journal for publication on this very subject. This research paper supported my teaching approach regarding putting emphasis on developing fundamental components in all areas of martial arts training.

A comprehensive approach to teaching martial art is very demanding on the instructor but the dividends are more than worth the effort. First of all, this teaching method introduces a variety of new things to classes, so the students are less likely to get bored. Secondly, the students and parents are able to see the evidence of their skills improving. Thirdly, the student retention rate stays high, which is great for business.

Lastly, the sense of accomplishment is enjoyed by both the students and the instructor. Though labor-intense, proper intervention of innovation leads to success.

Now that I have your full attention on the importance of technique execution, let's talk a little more about five stances that appear and coexist in nearly all the Taekwondo Poomsae (forms or patterns), whether WTF or ITF styles. In fact these same stances commonly coexist in most martial art forms irrespective of the system and style.

They are as follows:

- Natural Stance or Walking Stance
- Forward Stance
- Back Stance
- Cat Stance
- Horse Riding Stance (previously discussed – See Fig. 1 or 1a.)

Recalling my early days of martial arts training, the first thing that was taught was stances – learning what they were, how they differed from one another and understanding the application for each one. Students had a firm understanding of their stances before they were taught their first Kata (forms or patterns). (At that time, the word Poomsae had not been created, nor most of the terms currently used today.)

As some martial arts instruction progressed toward the sporting arena, the gap between the martial world and the sporting world widened, which led to emphasizing movement that supported a kicking-oriented style of combat with limited hand usage.

The WTF, in 2013, had begun to realize that the participation level of sports competitors was beginning to decline in both numbers and interest. Kukkiwon-qualified instructors were dispatched to all parts of the world to reaffirm the importance of technique execution and its relationship to Poomsae (forms or patterns) with emphasis on stances, blocks, strikes and, believe it or not, the shout or yell.

The main reason for the historical martial-based departure was the ambitious attempt to become an Olympic sport while distinguishing Taekwondo from its begrudged Karate roots.

Please examine the stance illustrations below for a comparative analysis in the variations of competitive (sport) versus martial applications. Let's take a closer look at each stance and its associated properties one at a time:

Fig. 6   *Fig. 2*

THE NATURAL STANCE (WALKING STANCE)

Competitive (Fig. 6) – stance is narrow
Martial (Fig. 2) – stance is slightly wider

Fig. 7

Fig. 3

THE FORWARD STANCE

Competitive (Fig. 7) – stance is narrow
Martial (Fig. 3) – stance is slightly wider and deeper

Fig. 8

Fig. 4

THE BACK STANCE

Competitive (Fig. 8) – stance is narrow
Martial (Fig. 4) – stance is wider and deeper

Fig. 9   *Fig. 5*

THE CAT STANCE (TIGER STANCE)

Competitive (Fig. 9) – stance is narrow
Martial (Fig. 5) – stance is slightly wider, longer and lower

Fig. 10   *Fig. 1*

THE HORSE STANCE (HORSE RIDING STANCE)

Competitive (Fig. 10) – stance is similar but not as low
Martial (Fig. 1) – stance is lower

From November 19 to 22, 2015, I participated in a Kukkiwon-sponsored 18th Poom/Dan Promotion Test Examiner Certification Course held in Chicago, Illinois in the United States. Kukkiwon-certified special Poomsae instructors, GM Jae Yoon Ahn and GM In Sik Hwang, offered detailed Poomsae instructions on both color belt *(youkeupja)* and black belt *(youdanja)*, respectively.

GM Ahn

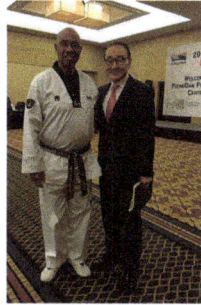

GM Hwang

The Kukkiwon-rank range of the participants was fourth Dan to eighth Dan masters from thirty-two American states and a few from various Canadian provinces. Both GM Ahn and GM Hwang (pictured above) continuously complained about poor stance skills of those participants who focus their dojang teaching on the sport of Taekwondo.

However, those participating masters that emphasized martial arts training in their dojang shone like stars in a moonless night. Those martial masters had other things in common: thirty-five plus years of training – often referred to as the 'old-school type' by the sport enthusiast.

It's also worth noting that, of the eighty million people that practice WTF Taekwondo, less than one percent participate in the sporting competition. One could obviously make a strong business case for WTF to redirect its focus on the martial arts and fitness components.

In view of the declining practice of WTF Taekwondo in Korea itself, federation officials have begun emphasizing the martial arts applications whenever Poomsae instruction is offered at Kukki-sponsored events, which oftentimes looks more like Karate. For us 'old-school types', WTF has gone full circle. It looks and feels like exactly what we were taught forty, fifty years ago.

When and how do I teach Stances at the Institute?

A proven successful teaching method for both children and adults is by making it fun. We call it the 'stepping game.'

I was in the United Arab Emirates at GM Zeyad Hammad Abu Zahieh's dojang. He too is considered 'old school' where basics are stressed. He had a stepping drill for his students to learn too. Funny as I think about it – you can visit the dojang of any 'old-school' master and observe that the teaching content is the same or very similar.

There are eleven-plus stances to be learned to support Poomsae and ten stances to support Shorin-Ryu karate martial training (Kata-based), which is also taught at the Institute.

This might seem like a lot but keep in mind that developmental drills add fundamental substance to the training process, whether it be martial- or sport-oriented.

Moreover, research has clearly identified how sound developmental movement drills dramatically improve cognitive regulation.

As an analogy, at birth, an infant first learns to breathe, then it learns how to drink and swallow, simultaneously. The newborn is not capable of walking. Many development components have to be learned and mastered and these components must be learned in both a chronological and incremental fashion. If a development stage is missed, other stages of development are adversely affected.

The same is true for martial arts training, irrespective of the athleticism of the student. This is a common error made by many instructors. Don't steal from your student's incremental progress. Basics first! Be patient.

Two of the Global Task Group's (GTG's) subject courses – Syllabus Creation and Building Lesson Plans – may be invaluable guides in this area of discussion.

BLOCKS

Like stances, the defensive or blocking aspect falls into the same category, for both the competitive (sport) and martial technique execution versions, as illustrated below.

From a casual glance, it's easy to see the competitive (sport) application method is mainly concerned with artistic presentation and speed, while the martial application employs the self-protection considerations: balance and stability.

The competitive (sport) application is concerned with the symmetry of body – arms, leg and foot positioning – while the martial application concentrates solely on functionality and effectiveness relative to a stable stance.

This will explain why the competitive (sport) blocking range of mechanical motion starts on the outside whereas the martial blocking is an inner-outer motion, making it more compact for a faster execution.

Please examine the blocks illustrations and definitions that follow for a comparative analysis of the variations of competitive (sport) versus martial applications. Let's take a closer look at each block and its associated properties one at a time:

THE LOW BLOCK

- Competitive (Figs. 13a, 13b) – this block starts at shoulder-height and travels downward across the body centreline, stopping in front of the knee, two fist-widths from the knee. Thus symmetrically aesthetic.
- Martial (Figs. 17a, 17b) – this block starts at shoulder-height and travels downward, stopping just left of body centreline. The rationale being that the attacking component has been redirected, thus allowing for an instantaneous counter reaction.

Fig. 13a   *Fig. 13b*   *Fig. 17a*   *Fig. 17b*

THE IN-TO-OUT BLOCK

- Competitive (Figs. 14a, 14b) – this block starts at mid-body, travels upward and across the body centreline, stopping directly in front of the shoulder at an angle of no more than 110 degrees. Thus symmetrically aesthetic.
- Martial (Figs. 18a, 18b) – this block starts in front of the body at mid-body, travels upward and across the body centreline, stopping just left of body centreline. Having redirected the attacking component, an instantaneous counter reaction can be executed. Note that the blocking hand is in a perfect position to quickly defend against

another attack by simply sliding the blocking hand to right of body centreline.

Fig. 14a　　　*Fig. 14b*　　　*Fig. 18a*　　　*Fig. 18b*

THE OUT-TO-IN BLOCK

- Competitive (Figs. 15a, 15b) – this block starts from the outer extremities of the body in an L-shape and travels inward, stopping directly in front of the shoulder at an angle of no more than 110 degrees. Thus symmetrically aesthetic.

- Martial (Figs. 19a, 19b) – the martial version of this block starts from the outer extremities of the body in a V-shape, travels inward crossing the body centreline and stopping just left of body centreline. The attacking component is redirected. Please note that the elbow starts in a down position, which reduces areas of vulnerability throughout the blocking transition motion. Here again, the blocking hand is in a perfect position to quickly defend against another attack by simply sliding to right of body centreline.

Fig. 15a   *Fig. 15b*   *Fig. 19a*   *Fig. 19b*

The Upper Block

- Competitive (Figs. 16a, 16b) – this block starts at mid-body, travels straight upward and stops slightly above the forehead. The blocking hand is positioned one fist-width in front of the forehead. Thus symmetrically aesthetic.

- Martial (Figs. 20a, 20b) – this block starts at mid-body, travels straight upward and stops well above the forehead. Please note that the travelling hand in this case is on the inside not the outside. Thus the concept of keeping a defending element between you and an attacker throughout the blocking transition motion is preserved.

Fig. 16a   *Fig. 16b*   *Fig. 20a*   *Fig. 20b*

The Master Instructor must have a clear understanding of these differences before he/she begins to teach their students and be able to determine which teaching approach is best suited for their students. From a purely sport-oriented Taekwondo school, the sports model is the only representation that a typical student gets. Poomsae is often taught as a grading requirement and has very little relevance to a student's self-defence skill development.

Being aware of these radical differences, what does the Master Instructor do?

Here comes the hard part: putting together a sustainable series of training modules and lesson plans that will provide predictable student development.

KICKS

The white-belter needs to concentrate on frontal movement, for example, push kick, front kick, crescent kick, axe kick, and then the round kick (turning kick). Simple basic kicks.

Yet embedded in those kicking mechanics lie the fundamental properties of movement, which coexist in all the other more advanced kicking techniques. Thus, you master the basics, you master the advanced.

First of all, what do I mean by the term 'mechanics'?

Remember, I was in the department of physics.

By definition, mechanics is the branch of physics that deals with the action of forces on bodies and with motion, comprised of kinetics, statics and kinematics: the technical aspect or working part.

Let's examine this concept by dissecting the mechanics of the push kick:

- You are standing on one leg.
- The knee of the other leg is raised to your chest (see Fig. 21).
- The leg is raised using the anterior muscles, such as the quadriceps; flex the thigh at the hip and extend the leg at the knee (see Fig. 21a).

- The hamstrings and gluteus maximus produce the opposite motion, extending the thigh at the hip and flexion of the leg at the knee pushing frontward.

Fig. 21

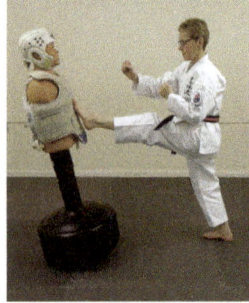

Fig. 21a

There is a tremendous amount of motion in action taking place here. It goes without saying: this basic kicking motion may require a lot of what I call skill cultivation.

THE MARTIAL KICK

The martial kick is very different from its sporting counterpart. Before we start to spend time drawing comparisons, let's examine the rationale behind these kicks and the philosophy supporting the displacement of the executed technique.

The anatomy – body structure and size – is a major consideration in empty-handed combat. It goes without saying that in the early days of martial arts development those factors were under consideration.

The physical size of the typical Okinawan is four feet and nine inches (145cm); an average Japanese is five feet and seven inches (170cm) and the typical Korean is five feet and nine inches (175cm).

So it's safe to say the Okinawans did not use their feet exclusively as a means of protection. The feet were used in collaboration with the hands, and vice versa. The feet targeted body parts from the abdomen region down and the hands targeted the upper body and head areas.

We all know the force that can be produced by the foot and leg. The round kick is a good example. It has the force potential of 950 foot-pounds. The execution of a spinning back kick is known to be capable of producing more than fifteen hundred foot-pounds of force.

Use of the hands explains the need for conditioning them

for heavy assault techniques. The makiwara served as a tool to assist with strengthening of the wrist, elbows, blade of the hands, fingertips and knuckles of the fist.

So executing a high kick in the open sky was not necessary, especially with those short legs. Evidence of this is repeatedly represented in Karate Kata and WTF-style Poomsae where ninety-eight percent of the kicking techniques target the abdomen region of the body. Might I add that Poomsae in the WTF style also targets most of its punches to the body.

After careful observation, it is quite surprising that the WTF style, which is known for its kicking, did not create a Poomsae series that represents its method of sport sparring, and it is also apparent that Poomsae and the sport sparring were developed independently of each other.

So I have a sneaking suspicion that the Poomsae is the WTF's martial arts model which requires fewer kicks.

Those kicks are:

FRONT – THIS KICK APPEARS IN THE FOLLOWING WTF POOMSAES:
- Colour Belt Poomsae
    1. Taeguek 1 through Taeguek 8
    2. Palgwe 2 and Palgwe 4 to Palgwe 7

(Please note that Palgwe Poomsae series is no longer officially recognized by WTF but is still taught at the Institute.)

- Black Belt Poomsae
    1. Koryo, Taebaek, Pyongwon, Shipjin, Jitae, Chonkwon, Hansu and Ilyeo

The front kick (Ap Chagi) is a very versatile kick. Depending on the flexibility of the student, this kick has a target range that starts at the knee joint and can extend to the head. The front kick, if barefooted, uses the ball of the foot as its primary instrument. This kick is virtually impossible to stop when used in counter means, close quarter engagements, and is ideal for follow-up hand attacking techniques.

ROUND – THIS KICK APPEARS IN THE FOLLOWING WTF POOMSAES:

- Colour Belt Poomsae
    1. Taeguek 6

- Black Belt Poomsae
    1. Koryo, Taebaek, Pyongwon, Shipjin, Jitae, Chonkwon, Hansu and Ilyeo

The round kick (Dollyo Chagi) is another versatile kick. Like the front kick, it too has a target range that starts at the knee joint and can extend to the head. The round kick has a power potential of nine hundred and fifty foot-pounds that can produce enough force to crack ribs or cause a concussion. It's a great tool when there is a height disadvantage.

The inverse of the round kick was historically known as the reverse round kick (Bandae Dollyo Chagi), and is the most revered and most dangerous of all the kicks used in the martial art world. The targeted area is the head and it happens to be the leg technique that has knocked out more competitors than any other kick. Its martial application can be lethal as the heel of the foot or shoe serves as the instrument of engagement. In competition the palm of the foot is used as it offers more reach.

SIDE – THIS KICK APPEARS IN THE FOLLOWING WTF POOMSAES:
- Colour Belt Poomsae
  1. Taeguek 4 and Taeguek 5
  2. Palgwe 5, Palgwe 6 and Palgwe 7

Please note that Palgwe Poomsae series is no longer officially recognized by WTF but is still taught at the Institute.)

- Black Belt Poomsae
  1. Koryo, Taebaek, Pyongwon, Jitae, Chonkwon, Hansu and Ilyeo

BACK – THIS KICK DOES NOT APPEAR IN THE ANY OF WTF POOMSAES.

The back kick (Dwit Chagi) and spinning back kick are two of the most devastating kicks. These two are primarily counter kicks with destructive outcomes when they connect with their target.

The back kick is an ideal self-defence tool for a multiple attacker situation.

The spinning back kick is the kick used in competition as a counter tool to round kick-initialized attacks.

Both of these kicks can yield forces exceeding fifteen hundred foot-pounds. So exactly what can fifteen hundred foot-pounds of force do to a body? Well, it can compress the chest cavity three to four inches, which can be deadly.

CRESCENT – THIS KICK APPEARS IN THE FOLLOWING WTF POOMSAES:

- Colour Belt Poomsae
  1. Taeguek 7
  2. Palgwe 7

(Please note that Palgwe Poomsae series is no longer officially recognized by WTF but is still taught at the Institute.)

- Black Belt Poomsae
  1. Chonkwon

The crescent kick (Anuroh Whoregi or Bandal Chagi) has two executable properties. One being a leg-swing with an outside-to-inside motion and the other is an inside-to-outside motion. The targeted area is usually the head.

The outside-to-inside motion uses the bottom or palm of the foot as the contact instrument.

The inside-to-outside motion uses the top area of the foot as the contact instrument.

A shortened motion of in-to-out variation is sometimes known as the 'twist kick' and is great for close-quarter engagements.

So forty, fifty years ago these were the primary kicks taught in martial art clubs and schools and executed in tournaments.

The Institute has twenty-eight kicks in its syllabus. Where did all those kicks come from?

They evolved out of the variation of competition play. As the athletes became more agile, faster, bigger and more flexible, more kicks were created as attacking and counter-attacking elements.

By the 1990s, WTF Taekwondo had become an Olympic sport. There was an all-out effort to stimulate the advancement of this kicking-oriented sport, leaving behind its martial roots.

As previously mentioned, professional Taekwondo sporting clubs have popped up all over the world to the extent that the sport of Taekwondo competition has become an arena for the gifted and elite athlete. This has led to a global decline in tournament participation, even in Korea, its birthplace.

Organizations like the Global Task Group Ltd (GTG) have recently surfaced in order to reconnect Taekwondo with its martial past by recapturing and embracing those martial elements that produce a rounded, balanced, individual fit to positively contribute to a better society.

A STUDY OF THE POWER
POTENTIAL OF POOMSAE

The Palgwe forms were introduced in 1967 by a committee, which had been formed in 1965 by the Korean Taekwondo Association. The committee was made up of:

- Kwak Gun Sik (Chung Do Kwan)
- Lee Young Sup (Song Moo Kwan)
- Lee Kyo Yun (Han Moo Kwan)
- Park Hae Man) (Chung Do Kwan)
- Hyun Jong Myun (Oh Do Kwan)
- Kim Soon Bae (Chang Moo Kwan).

After researching the martial art careers of the members of this committee, I discovered that all had a working knowledge of Kata practised by Shotokan and Shito Ryu karate styles (please see lineage Geno Chart on the final page of the book).

The Taegeuk Poomsae series was introduced in 1972 to replace the Palgwes and I can vividly recall being taught the Taegeuk forms by Grand Master Park Hae Man, one of their creators.

In spite of having been taught by one of the architects of

the forms, however, I find that every trip to South Korea results in my returning to Scotland and having to show my students changes that have been introduced. Students find this stressful, especially if they perceive that the new method of executing a technique appears to be less effective than the previous one.

It is particularly difficult for children to understand why these changes are necessary. I vividly recall a message I received from an Assistant Instructor during a recent trip to South Korea.

In fact, the message was not from the Instructor, it was from a seven-year-old student. She had asked the instructor to convey it to me. What she had said to the instructor was:

"Please, please, Miss, tell Sir no more changes!"

It isn't just the perplexing changes that can discourage dedicated Poomsae practitioners, I am sure that most of my readers will know the usefulness of the practice of Poomsae is disputed in some sections of the WTF Taekwondo world. This dispute hinges on its usefulness for real-life self-defence and fighting situations.

Last year (2015), I decided to conduct my own research into whether or not it is a waste of time for the martial artist to practise the Palgwe / Taegeuk series of Poomsae, by attempting to measure the amount of force produced by the techniques most commonly used in these two series of Poomsae. Determining the amount of force generated would allow me to make reasoned deductions about the potential harm inflicted on the body of an attacker by these techniques.

As you know, Taekwondo is a kick-oriented martial art. Both the Palgwe and Taeguek series of Poomsae emphasize the use of hand techniques. I decided to collect data to determine whether or not the kick is significantly more powerful than the punch. If I found from my data that it was, I planned to explore changing the Poomsae architecture by incorporating kicks in lieu of punches.

The data-gathering was carried out using fifty-eight students from the Traditional Taekwondo Martial Arts Institute. Unlike most studies of this nature, none of the participants were considered to be 'elite athletes'. None has ever competed in an 'elite' tournament.

Collectively, the participants in this project could be categorized as non-competitive Taekwondo practitioners with a primary interest in personal development, with focus on improving cognitive emotional regulation, stress relief, self-confidence, self-esteem and fitness for wellbeing.

The data that was gathered provided quantitative evidence that the lethality of all techniques improves with increased age, number of years of training, and most importantly, rank.

What is even more interesting is that the data also provides clear quantitative evidence that the most lethal techniques in all age or rank groups are kicks, especially the side kick, back kick, round kick and jump front kick.

This would seem to show that the focal point of any modification of the Poomsae should be the maximization of the use of these most lethal techniques in collaboration with hand techniques, especially for the middle-aged adult, due to limited flexibility ranges.

The data also supports the use of collaborative offensive consideration for adult practitioners, that is, kicks to the torso region and hand techniques to the upper torso region including the head.

Although a limitation of the study was that numerical results were normalized and could not be represented as 'real force units' (e.g. pound-force or Newtons), I believe they add weight to the notion that the martial art effectiveness of Poomsae could and should be increased.

This could be achieved by reform of the training curriculum including the creation of an effective Poomsae series that resembles WTF fighting style, or the creation of a practical self-defence techniques series that represents Poomsae applications.

This is one of the many areas that the GTG has set out to achieve. I want to be able to give to the next seven-year-old student who protests a very good rationale for changes made by being able to show how it will work to protect that student in a dangerous situation, rather than explaining how it looks nicer when presented in a competition.

Copies of this research paper have been sent to Kukkiwon's Research Department at the end of August 2015 and again in January this year, Unfortunately, unlike my two previous research papers, this one has not yet been published in the Kukkiwon Research Journal.

STANCE TRANSITIONS AND THEIR MARTIAL IMPORTANCE

The questions that all serious-minded Taekwondo Masters and Grand Masters should be asking themselves are:

- What is the martial significance of Poomsae practice, whether it be the Palgwe or Taeguek series?
- How important are the stances and displacement of punches and kicks?

With so much emphasis being put on the sport from a sparring perspective, the role and importance of Poomsae is often overlooked.

A case in point: the construction of a house starts with selecting the style. Once the style is determined, the next step is choosing the build site. The build site must support the style. If this condition is satisfied, the footing is laid.

Martial art training is no different.

The new student is typically interested in improving their fitness, or building confidence, or learning how to effectively protect themselves. Polling data collected for one of my published research papers has indicated that new students have collectively requested martial arts training.

So the new student is taught basic stances and how to manoeuvre from one stance to another. This is taught from the very start in conjunction with the Poomsae, be it Palgwe or Taeguek.

The Poomsae selected serves as the 'style', which is based on the student's physical properties, motor skills and cognitive fitness.

Stances definition was discussed earlier but I want to provide a little more detail. From the beginning of martial art training the importance of the stances is stressed. These stances are Walking Stance, Forward Stance, Back Stance, Horse Stance, and Cat Stance.

All these stances appear in both the Palgwe and Taeguek series of Poomsae.

However, some of these stances are used in Poomsae that the student does not learn for several months.

As an example, in Taegueks IL Jang (1), Yi Jang (2) and Sam Jang (3) all only use the Walking and Forward stances, while Palgwe 1 has the Walking Stance, Forward Stance and Back Stance.

A student taught only the Taegueks would not have a need for the Back Stance until they were nearly blue belt. And if the dojang they attend focuses only on Gyoroogi, the student may never learn the Back Stance at all. Nor the Horse Stance or Cat Stance for that matter.

So 'transition stance movement' would go undeveloped.

So just how do you assist the students in developing a thorough understanding of 'transition stance movement'?

Here's a suggestion that might be helpful.

First make sure that the students have a sound working knowledge of all the basic stances taught in your program and also how they differ.

Now let's create a 'stepping game'. Position all the students in a starting position stance with both feet parallel and close together. This stance is also known as Moa Seogi.

Moving only the left foot, position the students into the starting stance for every martial art movement, both feet parallel about shoulder-width apart. This stance is known as Narani Seogi.

On your command, have the students return back to the Moa Seogi position moving only the left foot.

On your command, have the students move only the left foot into a Horse Stance. This stance is known as Juchum Seogi. Then to Narani Seogi and finally back to Moa Seogi position.

Make sure to include all your basic stances in this stepping drill and do not forget to practise the right side too.

Practising those stepping drills on both sides increases the students' balance in movement and ensures 'stance step foot spacing' symmetry. When the stance step foot spacing is symmetrical, the student's finishing and starting points will be the same when performing their Poomsae. This is a critical factor in Poomsae competition and an incorrect finishing position will result in point deductions from the judges.

Employing this type of stance interaction will quickly and dramatically improve your students' 'transition stance movement'. These drills, if practised a few minutes at the beginning of each class, will lead to an attractive Poomsae presentation in a very short space of time.

Remember, make your classes fun!

The reader should begin to see the link between mastering stances, stance-to-stance manipulation and the practice of Poomsae.

Please note that the stances and their interconnection also correlate with kicks and punches that coexist in those Poomsae as well.

The students must be taught the importance of kick and punch displacement as well. The offensive components are not performed in an arbitrary manner but must be targeted to a specific section of the body in order to overpower or gain advantage over an opponent.

For another example, take a look at Taeguek Sam Jang (3). Embedded in this Poomsae is a Knife Hand Strike and a Knife Hand Block.

When did you teach your student how to execute a knife hand technique of any kind? Possibly the creation of blocking drills similar to the stepping drills would be an effective means of assisting the students to execute their blocks correctly.

All of these Poomsae elements should be taught independently of each other, weeks prior to the introduction of the actual Poomsae itself. The drills created can be performed static 'in space', on target apparatus, with partners and on the move, employing a variety of stances.

The students will find it fun and they serve as excellent technique development building blocks.

The Master Instructor is obliged to make the student aware of target offensive component displacement and to make them cognizant of the application when practicing Poomsae.

Self-defence drills can and should be created by extracting several Hoshin Sool elements from each and every Poomsae so that the student can repeatedly execute these, one after another, without hesitation.

I would encourage employing these Drills using multiple attack scenarios. These types of 'situation drills' can be real confidence builders.

Awareness of these individual components and how they interplay with one another will produce a much more energized Poomsae performance with sharp, distinguishable techniques. These Poomsae presentations will leave you and your students feeling both satisfied and accomplished.

KICKING, PUNCHING AND RAZZLE-DAZZLE

One important feature of Taekwondo is its free-fighting combat system, known as Gyoroogi, where bare hands and feet are used to repel an opponent. Persons trained in Taekwondo are possessed of a special kind of self-confidence in not only their physical ability but also their mental discipline. Taekwondo-trained individuals have developed techniques for personal defence by using their entire body: hands, fists, elbows, knees, feet and head.

Taekwondo practice, as a martial art form, consists of four components: Poomsae, Gyoroogi, Kyukpa and Hoshin Sool.

1. Poomsae is a line of movements based on traditional Far Eastern ideas of defensive and offensive martial tactics.
2. Gyoroogi is actual sparring between two people using defensive and offensive techniques.
3. Kyukpa means breaking. Practitioners train in breaking solid objects such as wooden planks and bricks.
4. Hoshin Sool means self-defence. The practitioner training is focused on disabling an opponent by attacking vital body parts.

This Korean-developed martial art is also enjoyed as a sport and loved by many in over two hundred and four countries.

A constitution, regulations and promotion tests have been well developed to meet the requirements for Taekwondo to be recognized as an International Amateur Sport.

Taekwondo made its debut as a full medal sport at the 2000 Olympic Games in Sydney.

Despite the dramatic global growth and popularity of Olympic Style Sport Taekwondo, an argument is ongoing about the continuing need to foster and develop its main element, the martial arts aspect. This should be handed down to the next generation of martial artists so that they are equipped with traditional values, skills and knowledge of the ancient martial way.

In the early days, military personnel stationed in both Okinawa, Japan and South Korea found the martial arts training fascinating, with all the varying styles and fighting strategies. Those military pioneers assisted in the spread of those various martial arts systems throughout the world by becoming instructors in their own countries to add to the growing numbers of Japanese and Korean immigrants who moved to countries such as the USA and Canada.

Just from South Korea alone, military servicemen were returning home having been exposed to several schools of martial philosophy or Kwans.

There were five original Taekwondo Kwans:

- Chung Do Kwan founded by Won Kuk Lee – studied Shotokan in Japan
- Jido Kwan formed by Chun Sang Sup – studied Shotokan in Japan

- Chang Moo Kwan – Lee Nam Suk – studied Shudokan Karate in Japan
- Moo Duk Kwan – founded by Hwang Kee
- Song Moo Kwan – Byung Jick Ro – studied Shotokan in Japan.

As time passed, the traditional culture of the martial arts, which originated in Okinawa and was taken to Japan and then to Korea, became both a martial art and a sport that can be enjoyed by children and adults of all ages.

Born out of respect and good manners, it follows the principles of peace and emphasizes mental training before technique.

But those variations in style, technique execution methods and philosophy gave rise to discord, conflict and division that is still apparent to this day.

One of those differences was and still is the interpretation and application of Hyungs or Poomsae.

The road to development is long, demanding and lonely at times and requires continuity of one's practice on a daily basis.

Having a knowledgeable Master Instructor is paramount but is becoming more difficult to find nowadays.

In today's society there are relatively fewer chances to encounter a life-threatening situation than when empty-handed defence systems were first developed. However, the inherent physical, psychological and spiritual properties that are embedded in their philosophical teaching and practices are of great benefit to today's stress-filled society.

This is because of a few major factors.

First and foremost is the disconnection with some of the

founding teachers and pioneers who were directly responsible for the martial art's cultivation, development and advancement. Added to this is the erosion of the Master– Student relationship with the creation of National Governing Organizations.

Second is the dilution and shortening of the training time and scaling down of technical requirements for legal, financial and safety reasons.

Third is the sporting aspect, which has led to the elimination of certain tactical defence strategies and technique execution styles forced by the use of electronic equipment.

INITIAL EVALUATION OF NEW STUDENTS

Assessment of a new student's capabilities is the first priority once he or she signs up for one of our programs. On day one, the student is asked to follow along with the class and try to do what he sees the other students doing.

This allows our instructional team to make a quick assessment of:

1. How quickly the new student adjusts to the new stimulation
2. The new student's cognitive skills – strengths/weaknesses
3. Balance
4. Range of motion
5. Flexibility
6. Coordination – eye–hand, eye–foot, eye–hand–foot
7. Level of fitness – stamina.

This information is systemically collected and stored in the new student's confidential database file. After the data is analyzed, a training approach is created with established monitoring checkpoints. These checkpoints are not belt gradings but serve as indicators of progression: did the team get it right?

Based on the collected data, the new student is directed to the training syllabus that best supports his/her immediate needs and interest. The newcomer is taught either the Palgwe or the Taeguek series of Poomsae in conjunction with classical Okinawan Shorin-Ryu Karate, with Kobudo taught in later stages of martial development.

With a teaching mentor assigned, the typical first four to six weeks for a new student would consist of learning stances, basic blocks (lower, middle & upper), basic terms and phrases (Korean and Japanese), Kihon Kata, Poomsae (Palgwe or Taeguek) and five basic kicks (push kick, front kick, crescent kick, axe kick and turning kick).

Basic callisthenics combined with strengthening exercising must be part of the new student's training regime if he/she hopes to skilfully execute the blocks, punches and kicks. Any weaknesses or deficits have to be addressed and a plan created that will meet the development needs of that particular student. Remember the data collected from the new student's initial class? Having a clear, well-defined development training curriculum becomes invaluable.

This newcomer is not the only student in the class. There are students at varying stages of both physical and martial development present. So your lesson plans have to be sophisticated enough to be enjoyable, interesting, challenging and demanding; but not overwhelming. Lessons must collectively meet the needs of each individual student.

Putting together a teaching approach package can be very difficult for the adolescent or adult who has been physically inactive, because verbal explanations must accompany the instruction, primarily because of the 'fear of injury' factor.

Those students aged four to eight have not learned to fear 'fear' yet, nor have they mastered the implications of verbal instruction. For these reasons the instructor must possess good technique demonstration skills as the little ones learn by following what they see.

Sounds like a lot for students as young as age four? Maybe so, but ninety-five percent of my students speak at least two languages at this age.

The Institute has a very robust syllabus. Since its inception, the Institute has preserved the identity of being a military-oriented training establishment whereby students are expected to be academically sound, upright in character, trustworthy, loyal to country and skilfully capable in both 'empty hand' and 'classical weapon' engagement.

Evidence from research studies has shown that students who are taught multiple languages at a very young age have the capacity for learning, absorbing and processing information at an incredible rate. Their minds are like a sponge!

As per the Institute's belt grading matrix, listed in the student handbook, after twenty to twenty-five training hours, the new student is eligible for rank advancement, with the first belt being yellow (white with yellow stripe for Little Tigers, as they are called at the Institute). An abbreviated syllabus has been created for the Tigers and is taught at a slower speed, allowing them to progress up the belt scale, thus ensuring they eventually meet the requirements of a full yellow belt. Once the Tigers reach this stage, the abbreviated syllabus is abandoned.

The teaching method employed is a 'building block'

approach, so consistency in attendance is a must. Students are taught and encouraged to set and complete personal, achievable goals. Classes are well structured yet game oriented, requiring interactive participation.

Apart from belt rank related requirements, there is no other visible totem. This allows the student to comfortably develop at his/her own pace without an external pressure. An assigned mentor is ever present, offering encouragement and instruction as needed. This practice is maintained even up to the advanced under-black belt stages of martial training. Strong bonding relationships within the Institute are created. I think that this bonding contributes to the Institute's high retention rate.

Maintaining a consistent student-to-instructor ratio is essential for achieving the desired martial development in each and every student – we leave no one behind!

When we lived in Seattle, one of the conventional practices of martial arts school owners was to invite other successful, well-respected, Master-ranked martial artists to your belt grading to serve as examiners; usually, no more than two at any particular grading. However, three independent examiners was the norm for students testing for black belt ranks. I would invite the likes of GM Leon Preston from the University of Washington, Master Troy Evans from Marysville, Master Rick Gordon from Tacoma, GM Tony Qumming from McCord Air Force Base, GM Bob Nicholls from White Center and Port Angeles, Washington, GM Chris Chong and Master Steve Lovric from Vancouver, BC.

I was also invited to serve on their grading panels.

Fresh eyes, warm words of encouragement, technical advice and professional cooperation brought objectivity to our martial arts programs while strengthening the bond between us. You must remember, just a few years earlier, we were competitors ourselves, often competing against each other.

After the grading was completed, we would have lunch or dinner and discuss the grading results. Suggestions, recommendations and business advice would be offered at these gatherings.

Collectively, we were an encyclopaedia of martial arts history and technical knowledge. We had spent years of our training under the direct instruction of our respective Korean Grand Masters, who themselves were well known and distinguished martial artists in their own country.

All of the examiners invited to the Institute had students who competed on a local, regional and national level. Grand Master Preston, Grand Master Chong and myself had students who competed on the International stage. We were members of the Pan American Taekwondo Union, which was made up of thirty-two countries, North and South America.

The three of us were also highly regarded national referees and national coaches, having had to participate in a battery of instructional training courses on these subjects that began in the early days at the local and regional levels. In fact, Grand Master Chong became the Canadian National Team Coach and Grand Master Preston became the prestigious International Referee (IR) Chairman whose primary duty was to conduct International Referee seminars for the World Taekwondo Federation (WTF) in all two hundred and four national member associations, spanning five continents.

I became an international spokesperson and lecturer for

the Kukkiwon, the educational wing of the World Taekwondo Federation (WTF).

Sitting around a dinner table exchanging teaching concepts and training methods was extremely fruitful and enlightening. More often than not, I implemented the information collected at these dinner sessions almost immediately into the Institute's program. This information allowed me to fine-tune every aspect of my program, from syllabus refinement to the latest technical manoeuvres. I began to realize the importance of teaching stage development. As an example, I would not teach a white-belter spinning or turning kicks. *(Please note that the recently created Poom/Dan Examiners' Certification course incorporates the system we had in place many years ago. We continued to follow the procedures that our instructor had taught us.)*

TEACHING METHODS

Many times I have advised other masters, while reminding myself:

> *"Never teach world-class techniques to students who do not have world-class skills. You will never achieve the desired result. Focus on mastering the basics."*

This reminds me of an interview I had with a recruiter from IBM while in university. His name was David Crockett. During the interview he asked my Grade Point Average (GPA). I responded with embarrassment: "Three point four". I was in university with some brilliant guys. He replied, "Very good".

He then asked, "Are there more 'A' students than 'C' students?" I immediately answered, "No! It's just the opposite."

He agreed, and added, "The 'C' student will more than likely be the manager of the 'A' student."

Why?

Because there are more of them!

So the elite athletes, with those world-class skills, are few in number, like the academically exceptional student.

I had a successful interview with Mr Crockett. Weeks later, I received a letter inviting me to another interview but this time it included an all-expenses-paid flight to IBM's plant in Lexington, Kentucky.

Wow! My very first flight on an airplane. This was amazing stuff. This was the period in American history where bright, talented and educated Afro-Americans were heavily sought after by Fortune 500 companies. Companies like IBM and Honeywell took the lead in recruiting promising candidates with math, business and technical degrees. Those were exciting times and we were 'ascending stars', anxiously anticipating those new career opportunities.

Returning to the subject of teaching methods, I use a variety of instructional methods in order to ensure that I am responding to the needs of all of my students so that everyone masters these basics, not just the talented athlete:

The *direct instruction* method is probably the teaching strategy that we are most familiar with from our own experience in the classroom and the dojang / dojo. With this method it is the instructor who decides what is important for the students to do and specifically explains or demonstrates a skill or technique. The student attempts to replicate the technique, a process that requires focus and concentration but minimal understanding or analysis.

This is when a well-structured and organized training syllabus is critical!

I vividly recall observing many masters allowing new students to perform advanced techniques.

The Institute's requirements to advance from white belt to yellow belt includes time-in-grade (twenty-five training hours) and the following, listed on the next page and shown in Table 1 on page 185 (and these are the only items taught to them regardless of personal skill levels):

1. Four basic blocks
   - Low block
   - In-to-out block
   - Out-to-in block
   - Upper block

2. Five basic kicks
   - Push kick
   - Front kick
   - Crescent kick
   - Axe kick
   - Round kick

   i. Punching from a horse stance
   ii. Reciting greetings, basic terms and phrases
   iii. Reciting school's motto
   iv. Reciting Taekwondo tenets
   v. Submitting an essay: 'What is Respect?'

The Institute's requirements to advance from yellow belt to yellow with green stripe belt includes time-in-grade (twenty-five training hours) and the following listed and shown in the Table 1 on page 185:

3. Four basic blocks
   - Low block
   - In-to-out block
   - Out-to-in block
   - Upper block

4. Additional blocks
   - Knife Hand block (In-to-out)
   - Knife Hand block (Out-to-in)

5. Five basic kicks
   - Push kick
   - Front kick
   - Crescent kick
   - Axe kick
   - Round kick

6. Additional kicks
   - Side kick
   - Back kick
   - Turning back kick

i.   Punching from a horse stance
ii. Reciting greetings, basic terms and phrases
iii. Reciting school's motto
iv. Reciting Taekwondo tenets
v.   Submitting an essay: 'Ethics & Morality'.

The Institute's requirements to advance from yellow with green stripe to green belt includes time-in-grade (thirty training hours minimum), all the requirements of the green stripe, and at this stage the green belt candidate test is conducted in both Japanese and Korean where applicable. See rank requirements shown in Table 1 on page 186.

These grading requirements are levied on all students irrespective of their athleticism or physical abilities. They must all be taught the same developmental elements to ensure educational continuity.

DRILL AND PRACTICE

The students are required to practise the skills and techniques that have already been learned in order to help them to remember what they have been taught, as well as to hone and improve the skills. For example, one Friday night at Bannatyne's Health club, where I give lessons, the lesson for that particular session focused on the execution of the side kick. The entire two-hour session was devoted to side kicking with emphasis placed on the knee displacement mechanics and the thrusting movement of the hips.

The target-attack area was knee level using front leg and rear leg assault drills.

With the focused attack area being so low, subliminally the student was also improving their one-legged balance.

By the end of the class, the participants were able to execute the kick at mid-body with improved and stable balance and with accuracy using hip-action power.

LECTURES AND SEMINARS

I use this method when I wish to convey a large amount of information in a short amount of time. I have arranged seminars on the history of martial arts in order to give students knowledge about their traditions and lineage. I am concerned with teaching the whole package, not just a part of it. This is the teaching approach that I learned from GM Kwon and it remains a very useful tool in my toolbox of teaching approaches.

QUESTION AND ANSWER

Asking students questions allows me to assess students' recall of what has been previously taught. I use the 'question and answer' teaching method in order to give students the opportunity to apply previous information to what they are currently learning so that their understanding deepens. I also encourage my students to go away and think about what they have learned and then come back to class and ask me questions. This encourages them to apply new knowledge and use that as a basis for synthesizing new knowledge. Promoting creative thinking on the part of the student empowers the student and helps them to take personal responsibility for their own learning, but it also means that the instructor must be knowledgeable about his subject yet willing to admit that he does not know all the answers. I often contact Hanshi to check my understanding when my students ask challenging questions.

DISCOVERY-LEARNING

The discovery-learning approach involves the provision of group activities that allow students to find learning for themselves. Discovery-learning allows students to engage in the activity and see for themselves what happens when they apply what they have been learning, or not, as the case may be. As a result, students learn how to personalize their martial art and make a technique his/her own. This is where it is essential to have a number of trained assistants available to provide supervision and structure.

There is a lot to be learned from simply mastering the basics but effectively teaching the basics requires innovation and flexibility on the part of the instructor.

I am not going to break down each and every component of kicking, blocking or striking. I merely wish to make the reader – be he/she a martial artist or Master Instructor – cognizant of teaching considerations that can ultimately lead to well-trained and able students who have become both effective thinkers and individuals who are capable of efficiently defending themselves.

There are quite a few teaching methods – probably as many as there are ways of learning – and I have only mentioned a few of them. Like a teacher in a secondary school, the instructor must be consistently aware of his audience, his students. He must be totally aware of their learning capacity, their learning rate. In other words, their cognitive skills. Their physical attributes must also be kept under the microscope.

Years ago, education majors in university had to take a two-semester course entitled 'Testing Measurement'. This coursework armed the soon-to-be teacher with the tools for monitoring, measuring and testing his/her pupils.

Most martial arts instructors are clueless in these areas. I think that there is a perceived disconnection of martial arts instructors from their academic institution-oriented counterparts. This should not be the case; they are teachers too! This means that they must adhere to the same criteria of regular attendance and participation in seminars that give insight into changes in their chosen profession. Moreover, it should be a requirement for rank advancement.

Teaching is an occupation and a profession.

However, the mindset can be completely different with martial art instruction. As an occupation, financial considerations are at the forefront. It's about making money and doing things that generate income. Dojangs are strategically situated in areas of a city were personal income is highest and where the ability to pay is assured. The Master Instructor can either be part-time (employed somewhere else during hte day), or full-time (classes taught throughout the day). In recent years, class instruction times have been cut to forty-five minute sessions twice a week, even for adults. Additional program-specific instruction is available under a different program package – for more money.

As an example, would you find it acceptable for your child's secondary math teacher to reduce the class time to forty-five minutes? No, you wouldn't! You would make an immediate visit to the school board to file a complaint.

Student development, whether academic or athletic, demands a professional approach where the focus is on cultivating the product through dedicated nurturing. As a professional, the Master Instructor is committed to growth and refinement of the product, the student.

What is needed is a profession that is professional.

On the top of the front page of the Institute's website we state:

"Our Business: Developing good martial artists, at a profit, if we can, at a loss, if we must. But always good martial artists!"

Now that the Master Instructor is clear as to his/her teaching methods, the next hurdle is creating a sustainable yet flexible lesson plan.

At the Institute, we use a 'backwards design' lesson plan approach. Allow me to explain. We first identify the desired result (objective). Then we determine the acceptable evidence (assessment) and finally, a plan of action within a defined period of performance (the actual lesson within a realistic time frame).

Backward designing is thinking about the:

Objectives of the lesson
- Assessment, i.e. how will the student prove he/she has achieved the objectives you set?
- Establishment of a realistic time frame.

A good lesson includes:
- Objectives
- Performance indicators
- Task analysis (new skills)
- Pre-assessment, skill, capabilities, etc., (know your audience)
- Resources (equipment)
- Instructional methods (are you teaching what you are assessing?)
- Warm-ups
- Core activities
- Cool-down
- Closure.

Wow! That's a lot of work, you are saying to yourself.

Not if you have the right tools for the job. I have a question for you: how long do you expect your clients to continue investing money, month after month, for forty-five minute sessions twice a week, for a mediocre product?

We are addressing the 'equity' of your occupation/profession. You're investing time and effort in the production of a product. Your clients are purchasing the product that you are advertising. So the task at hand must be to systematically stage your product development process in such a fashion that it meets local, regional and national standards.

I recently read a book entitled *Good to Great* by Jim Collins.

This book draws the readers' attention to how a good company becomes a great company. It also mentions the notable shortcomings that lead a good company to become a mediocre one, as well as the factors that inhibit a good company from becoming a great company.

Apathy is deadly!

Having skills and talented athletes will not lead to a successful program either. One only has to look at any professional sports league to see that that's not totally true. Take for example Manchester United's soccer team led by Alex Ferguson. He led a very successful program for years, dominating the league. Upon his retirement a few years ago, he left the team at the top of the league.

A new, equally well-known and gifted head coach was found and employed, with no changes to the team roster. When the new season started, Manchester United lost its first three games and the entire season was up and down, with more downs then ups. After a few seasons yielding similar results, a new coach was found, then another and still another. What happened?

The team was laced with young, talented, ambitious players with an historical winning track record. A team that played together as a unit for years. Could one person make a difference – the coach? Absolutely!!!

But it is not the coach as a position. Rather, it's the attributes that the coach possesses!

His/her speech pattern.

It's his/her choice of words.

His/her organizational skills.

It's his/her approach to the games.

It's his/her preparation methods.

It's his/her personality.

It's his/her ability to motivate, encourage, inspire.

Hanshi Frank Hargrove, my karate teacher for forty-two years, once told me: "David make sure that you touch each and every student that attends your classes each time that they attend." He didn't mean physically touch. What he meant was, offer gentle words of encouragement, advice, instruction, a piece of yourself that they can hold onto.

Another factor mentioned in the book *Good to Great* was

improvement in the procedures of the product development process. For example, in the case of teaching a new kick. Teach the kick and offer the application as part of the learning session. You can also create a variety of 'situation drills' that support the applications. This gives the student options and allows them to establish preferences. This is what I call personal technique identity: making it yours!

The student soon learns how to employ this new kick using a paddle, kick shield, or a heavy bag or even 'in space' (the absence of a physical target).

Still another most important piece of the successful program puzzle is stressing team unity. There is no 'I' in the word 'team'.

Incorporating the team concept in our program has been a major component of our success. Sometimes a totem can exist in a martial art school that has nothing to do with rank, for example, an athletically gifted student may consider himself superior to other students. The teaching methods employed at the Institute will not support the development of such a totem which could be the result of free sparring training. The spirit of teamwork is paramount in the Institute Martial Arts program.

Hanshi Hargrove's dojo was filled with marines, so the training was demanding and hard. This is the most polite way of describing it. It is from those marines that I learned the power of teamwork – working as one body, one unit. Success and failure is based on the strength of the weakest member of the team. So all have to be strong. If one wins, we all win. Students at the Institute realize that they are expected to be their best.

As a youth, one of my favourite college football teams was the Fighting Irish of Notre Dame located in South Bend,

Indiana. I adopted their team motto: "First you will be your best, then you will be first" (Knute Rockne, head coach of the Fighting Irish, 1918-1930).

This means that you will train tremendously hard to be your individual best. You must understand: most folks don't want to work that hard!

These concepts, teaching approaches and methods are introduced gradually and very subtly over a period of time in core class sessions as well as extended training sessions that include a variety of seminars and competition preparation training sessions.

THE IMPORTANCE OF GOOD COMMUNICATION SKILLS

When I moved to Scotland with my wife and young son in 1998 I knew it wouldn't be plain sailing and that I would encounter challenges, one of the first being the fact that I was considered overqualified for the jobs I applied for. The title 'Engineer' seemed to me to be used indiscriminately for washing machine repairmen, electricians and many other jobs that did not require a degree.

Everything was small – the houses were small, the garages were small and the portions in restaurants were tiny compared to the States. One thing I didn't expect to be a problem though was communication. I spoke the same language after all! Or did I? Everywhere I went I encountered baffled looks on the faces of many of the people I spoke to. Their expressions were nothing like the expression that came over my face when people attempted to communicate with me.

The common dialect in the north-east of Scotland is 'doric' and I found it almost impossible to figure out what was being said. I dreaded the arrival of a repairman to fix some piece of equipment in my house and delegated this task to my wife, Nicky.

The telephone was the worst and I quickly gave up answering our house phone, again delegating to Nicky. Every day I relayed whole conversations or the pieces of conversation that I could remember to her or one of her family so that they could explain to me what the conversation had been about. I would quickly have become rather isolated if I had not worked to open my martial art school as soon as possible.

When I opened up my dojang, however, I soon found myself being confronted with a roomful of puzzled faces in response to some of the instructions I gave. When I asked what the problem was, I couldn't understand the answer they gave me. Nicky came to my rescue and acted as interpreter between me and the students.

I realized that I would have to focus on my communication and listening skills if I was going to be able to conduct classes unaided. On one occasion I remember telling the students to use some 'head and shoulders'. Some of the students looked perplexed so I asked if they knew what 'head and shoulders' was. The prompt reply from one student was, "It's a shampoo, Sir!" So I learned to check out carefully if the students understood the instructions I had given them before commencing any activity. It is dangerous to make assumptions at any time but in a martial art school making assumptions can result in serious injuries and obviously I wanted to avoid this.

The accents and dialects placed a lot of demand on my listening skills and I really had to work on these. I had to develop more ability to listen patiently, to ask questions when I wasn't sure about something but not to interrupt when someone was speaking.

Biting my tongue and concentrating intensely does not come easily to me, especially if I think the speaker is saying something foolish, but I try to persevere. Another behavior that affects communication that I try to avoid is known as the 'rehearsal effect'.

This occurs when you are thinking about what you are going to say when it is your turn to speak, rather than listening to what is being said. You only hear a part of what has been said. This can lead to misunderstandings and conflict. In addition, people know when they are not being listened to and this can lead to hurt feelings and the stifling of further communication. Students may become reluctant to question when instructions are unclear to them, resulting in confusion and errors. I try to keep in mind that I have been given two ears but only one mouth for a reason.

It wasn't very long after I moved to Scotland that I discovered some significant cultural differences that I had been unaware of and would need to adapt to. My voice, for example was too loud for many people who thought I was shouting and being aggressive.

As well as this, Scottish people are protective of their personal space and standing too close to them when having a conversation was seen as invading that personal space. I had to learn to keep more distance between myself and the person I was talking to, but also to lower my voice a little so that I was still speaking audibly and clearly, but not so loudly that people felt intimidated. The personal space issue can cause headaches when teaching sparring techniques to students, however. I have often had to point out that the student and his or her partner are too far apart to reach each other with a kick, and a hand technique would have no chance at all. It is something some continue to struggle with and which needs regular reminders.

Many of the challenges I have encountered in Scotland I was not prepared for, even though my wife is Scottish but, in spite of these challenges and struggles, my teaching efforts have produced some very good students of whom I am justifiably proud.

Some have embarked on or completed degrees and others have received job promotions. On a personal note, I have been given the opportunity to demonstrate to my students from my own experience how, with perseverance and determination, challenges can be faced up to and overcome.

So, in a lot of ways, I am grateful for the stumbling blocks I have encountered in Scotland as they have come hand in hand with opportunities to assist my students in their personal development.

I also remind myself on a daily basis that many pioneering martial artists have left their homes to teach their skills in countries throughout the world so that more people could share in the benefits of the training and learning.

What was good enough for them must surely be good enough for me!

THE IMPORTANCE OF GOOD ASSISTANT INSTRUCTORS

Having a well-trained instructional staff is invaluable with all students, whatever their rank or skill level.

I can vividly recall opening and operating my first dojang. I had a surprisingly large number of new students. The enrolment rate seemed to happen in clusters, four or five at a time. It quickly became apparent that I would soon need a few good, trained assistants. But under what criteria would I select them and, once selected, what would I teach them? How would I teach them?

Occupationally I was employed at Boeing Aerospace as lead design electrical engineer – an industry where 'configuration control' is paramount! And that was the concept that I needed for my dojang operation too. My dojang had to function in such a manner that the instructional staff:

- were articulate in speech
- possessed good manners
- had the same speech pattern
- were armed with good presentation skills
- had a calming presence
- most importantly, had a willingness to learn and share knowledge.

So twenty-five years ago, on a Sunday afternoon, I set about drafting an instructor training outline which became a nine-module Assistant Instructor Training Manual that I still use to this day, incorporating updates where applicable from time to time.

Here again the GTG Masters Instruction course can provide helpful ideas for staff selection and training.

The Institute in Scotland has a large student population, all praise be to God. It goes without saying, the skill levels amongst those students vary tremendously. In order to ensure that each individual is given the nourishment appropriate to their needs, assistants are required. These must be *well-trained assistants*! Not simply students who have earned a black belt. Some of my assistants are currently red belts. I liken the Assistant Instructor Training Program, which all of my instructors and assistant instructors are required to attend, to the Officers Training Corp (OTC). The candidates are hand-picked, meeting selection requirements such as a willingness to learn, a desire to teach, integrity, loyalty, possessing a strong sense of purpose, knowledge of the syllabus and a visibly indomitable spirit!

Assistant instructors should be identified from amongst those students who have shown that they have not only leadership skills, but also the respect and understanding to follow their teacher's lead. Arrogance on the part of the instructor will lead to disenchanted students with poor skills, deviation from the syllabus and damage to the reputation of the school. They need to be humble enough to understand that their role as assistant instructors is about the students, not about them. They should also be committed to preserving the integrity of the school and its syllabus by only teaching what they have been taught.

The martial art lineage can then be preserved. It is the head instructor's responsibility to provide adequate training to ensure instructors and assistant instructors are competent to teach and deliver training as well as being technically competent in the martial art. They are, after all, the true Ambassadors of the Institute. Best practice is to create an Assistant Instructor's Program that supports them to develop the technical knowledge and leadership skills that they need in their instructor role.

My Assistant Instructor Program which I created all those years ago while I was living in Seattle, is the same program I use today. The nine training modules are:

- Module 1 – Leadership, Protection & Security
- Module 2 – Basic Developmental Training Skills, Level 1
- Module 3 – First Aid & Health
- Module 4 – Basic Developmental Training Skills, Level 2
- Module 5 – Referee and Judging Competition Training
- Module 6 – Intermediate Developmental Training Skills, Level 1
- Module 7 – Intermediate Developmental Training Skills, Level 2 (for instructors at Satellite Program Sites)
- Module 8 – Black Belt Training Seminar 1 (for instructors at Satellite Program Sites)
- Module 9 – Black Belt Training Seminar 2 (for instructors at Satellite Program Sites).

This training program, which includes written examinations, tests the assistant instructor candidates' desire to teach and their commitment to maintaining a respectworthy approach to their teaching role. They will need to demonstrate to lower-ranked students that they are worthy of being followed. That doesn't mean they should be expected to know it all but they do need to be seen to be constantly learning and improving.

ESSENTIAL INSTRUCTOR SKILLS

I believe that it is essential that every martial art instructor is a positive role model for his/her students. I am always mindful in every aspect of my life to consider whether or not my actions are those that I would wish my students to imitate. This is why I do not smoke or drink alcohol. Both of these are detrimental to health and costly. In addition, alcohol consumption can negatively impact on an individual's morality. A clear set of values that are lived in their personal life as well as in the dojang will encourage students to live in a way that supports their own personal beliefs and values. As already mentioned, arrogance and a focus on 'me' will be viewed negatively by students. Students need to believe that their instructor cares about them and their development. They are also likely to have more respect for, and confidence in, an instructor who shows commitment to family, his community, and his church. Role models should also have a passion for what they are doing and the desire and ability to communicate this passion to their students in a way that infects them.

It is also important that the instructor is accepting of all students whatever their class, religion, social or financial status. The instructor must be blind to all of these, focusing only on the student's needs and how he can assist with his/ her development. The ability to overcome obstacles in life as well as in the dojang is another way in which the instructor can act as a role model for his students. If students know that the instructor has overcome difficulties to reach his position in life as well as in martial art, they will be more willing to accept that they too can overcome obstacles to living a self-fulfilled, compassionate and caring life. Respect is a two-way street. If an instructor wishes to be respected by his students he needs to reciprocate and demonstrate that he is respecting of them. Classes should be started on time! Students have a life outside the dojang and are trying to fit their martial art training into a busy day – school, homework and study for younger students; work, family and other commitments for older students. If they cannot rely on the instructor to be respectful of their time, they will assign less value to the instructor and the school. Reliability and respect will pay dividends in terms of student referrals, class spirit and students' dedication to training.

I had planned to talk a little about the necessity of good time management skills on the part of the instructor at this point but, thinking about it, can anyone actually manage time? Can we somehow arrange to have a twenty-five or twenty-six hour day? No, of course we can't, so it makes more sense to say that we need to be able to manage ourselves, our resources and those activities or tasks that we need to complete within a designated time span. All of us have competing demands on our time: job, family responsibilities, community activities, social life, and it would be all too easy to get into the habit of rushing into the dojang two minutes before class is due to start without any definite idea of what we are going to teach. What effect would that have on our students? They would very quickly realize that their instructor is disorganized, lacking in self-discipline and not fully focused on what he is doing. At the same time he is asking students to pay attention to what he is saying, focus on the correct execution of techniques, and to show respect and self-discipline outside as well as inside the dojang. This 'do as I say, not as I do' approach would quickly empty the dojang and leave us wondering what had gone wrong.

Fairness and consistency are also important qualities a good instructor should demonstrate. Some students have more skills than others. The instructor needs to be careful to show that each and every student is valued and that the instructor believes that, whatever skill level the student may have, it can be developed and improved. Spending more time with the skilful student will result in others not feeling valued. Students will notice quickly and will not remain long if this is the case. Finally, I must stress the importance of the instructor remaining a student. The day an instructor stops thinking of him/herself as a student of martial arts is the day their techniques become stale and their spirit is diminished. As a result, the spirit in the school begins to die. However many years a martial artist has been training, there's always room for growth. After all, who would want to learn from someone who has given up on learning?

So we need to be mindful of our role-model position and impose the same self-discipline on our learning, teaching and dojang management that we expect from our students. Do you wing it or do you plan your lessons? If you do not use lesson plans, consider this…to begin with the end in mind means to start with a clear understanding of your destination. It means you know where you're going… so the steps you take are always in the right direction.

LESSON PLANNING

Not having a lesson plan is like setting out on a trip and not knowing where you are going or how you will know when you get there.

The success of my lessons and ultimately my school will be determined not only by how well they meet my personal martial art instructor goals, but by how well I manage to match my lessons to the goals and backgrounds of my students.

For me a good lesson plan needs to include all of the following:

1. Pre-assessment – I need to know my audience and the answers to questions such as:
   - who are the students – age, gender, background?
   - what are their motivations for joining my program?
   - what do the students already know and understand?
   - how do the students learn best?
   - what modifications in instruction might I need to make?

2. Objectives – what is it that I want to accomplish by the end of this class?
3. Performance indicators – what will the students be able to do at the end of the class that will show I have been successful?

4. Task analysis – task analysis is the process of taking a chained task and breaking it up into teachable components or a set of discrete steps. Unless we are aware of all the different parts of a given skill/concept, we can't effectively teach it to our students.

5. Resources – equipment and assistants. All equipment to be used needs to be checked for safety and be on hand ready for use. I need to know which assistants will be in class and available to assist.

6. Instructional methods – I have heard that teaching is like fishing… you use different lures for different fish and I use different teaching methods for different students. The teaching method or methods I will use for that particular class depends on factors such as the size of the class, the content and purpose of the lesson.

7. Delegated activities – delegating some aspects of the lesson to good assistant instructors allows me to focus on the things that only I have the expertise to teach. Some people do not like to delegate, as they are afraid that it will not be done properly, but if you have trained the assistants by showing them how you want to have things done, all should be well. Choose what tasks you want to delegate. Some will be better equipped for certain tasks than others. Train them and then trust them to do the job. Oh and don't forget to say "thank you"!

8. Warm-up – the purpose of a warm-up is to prepare the students' muscles for the efforts to be made in the class so it progresses from a general warm-up to a specific warm-up geared to that specific lesson.

9. Core activities – these are the specific activities that the

students will perform that will improve different aspects of their martial art. They can include blocking drills, kicking drills, Poomsae etc.

10. Cool-down – the body needs to recover after a strenuous workout and the cool-down can include activities such as stretching.

11. Closure – giving and receiving feedback on the lesson should not be forgotten.

After the students have gone home I reflect on the lesson and discuss it with the assistants who were present. What went well in the lesson? What problems did I experience? Are there things I could have done differently? How can I build on this lesson to make future lessons successful? How do the assistant instructors feel they coped with the activities delegated to them? I make sure that each assistant gives me feedback on the performance of the students they were supervising. It is my responsibility to have a good understanding of the progress of every student in the school so no student is handed over to an assistant and then forgotten. I make a point of ensuring that I spend time with all of my students, not just a chosen few.

MY FIRST UNIQUE TEACHING OPPORTUNITY

I had not long opened my first commercial site off of 308th Street in Federal Way Washington when a young female, accompanied by her mother, walked into the dojang one late afternoon. The mother was interested in self-defence training for her teenage daughter. I could tell by the manner in which they entered that they had money and they knew all they needed to know about the martial art schools in the area, which aided in their decision to train at the Institute. The young lady joined the program. Her name was Sarah.

Weeks passed and Sarah was progressing just fine. Shortly after her belt test for yellow belt, Sarah and her mother came into the dojang on Saturday morning with a young man who could not have been more than a couple of years older then Sarah. It was her older brother. He was home for the weekend. He was attending school somewhere near Portland, Oregon. It was a school for the blind. The young man was totally blind – from birth.

Sarah's mother wanted me to consider teaching her son martial arts, too.

Oh man, what a challenge!

Where do you start? How do you teach someone to do something they have never seen, or illustrate a technique without a shared reference point?

So I blindfolded myself in an attempt to learn what a blind person would feel and to try to determine what tools were used to navigate the world

This took me back to the days when I was in university. One of our professors who taught philosophy and religion had been blind from birth. He never experienced any problems moving around the campus from building to building. I recall a classmate asking him how he got around so easily. How did he know where he was?

He replied, "Each building has a different smell and sound, and the air pressure on my cheeks also helps to determine my location." Being in or near the cafeteria was obvious. However, when entering the science building he could smell chemicals. A hallway that connected to an exit had a different air pressure on the cheek than a hallway that connected to another hallway.

So I started trying to define what I was sensing while sitting in a chair with a blindfold on. I also walked around the dojang in an effort to understand what my senses were telling me:

What did I hear?

What did I smell?

What did I feel?

What did I sense?

I even took it to another level by blindfolding my students, one at a time, and asking them to perform Poomsae, or certain kicks, and observing their movements.

My observation lead to the realization that martial arts includes those things that you cannot see.

My students even to this day occasionally practice their Poomsae and Kata blindfolded.

Sarah's brother never enrolled in my program but the possibility of his enrolment, coupled with what I learned from my experiments, enlightened and broadened my comprehension of what is required to teach and prepare my students to become the best that they can be.

So when Sheila brought her grandson to my 2010 summer camp and suggested that she might want to join our program herself, I did not hesitate in extending an invitation.

Sheila had bilateral above-knee leg amputations.

Like in the case of Sarah's brother, I experimented with sitting in a chair to determine what were the limitations as well as the advantages from a seated position. I began planning how I could teach everything that was in my syllabus to someone from a seated position.

I first examined the areas of defence. What considerations had to be made in order to teach all the blocks? My first discovery was that the low block was not needed. I further discovered a method of punching that would support someone in a seated position. I also devised a variety of hand technique manipulations to replace kicking.

With this newfound knowledge, I created a series of drills that could comfortably be performed from a seated position and that could be integrated into the class so that they would benefit all of the students.

This led to the creation of adapted Poomsae specifically for students in a seated posture.

When practising self-defence skills, Sheila's opponents were all able-bodied.

When I took a team of competitors to Chicago in 2012 to participate in the USNTF/WTC International Taekwondo Championship, Sheila was part of that team.

She won Gold Medals in both Poomsae and Kyukpa and received a standing ovation from the audience.

Sheila earned the rank of 6th Keup before illness forced her to discontinue her training. Sadly she passed away shortly after that.

KEEPING NEW STUDENTS
FOCUSED AND ENGAGED

I have already referred to the first two months of training in a martial arts program as a critical time for the new student, and the input of a mentor is indispensable.

New students can quickly become bored practising the same techniques at every class, especially when they casually observe more advanced techniques being performed by other students.

At the Institute, the mentors who are assigned to the new student provide stimulating activities that keep the new student fully occupied and allow him or her to build the skills essential for the introduction to the core syllabus.

This includes stepping drills, blocking drills and kicking drills.

So what's wrong with teaching an athletic, enthusiastic white belt a jump spinning back kick?

It's wrong because basic movement, balance and agility have not been developed. I liken it to trying to get a six-week-old baby to eat solid food. Being allowed to make shortcuts in the developmental process will also leave them deficient in the areas of discipline and perseverance. Such students are likely to learn only the things that they find exciting and to reject those lessons that they really need.

So keeping new students motivated and absorbed whilst they work on those basic techniques that they need to learn requires planning, innovation and creativity, but obviously all students need to be motivated to work hard and produce the best results that they can. There are two types of motivation: extrinsic motivation and intrinsic motivation.

Extrinsic sources of motivation for martial art students may include:

- a new belt
- a medal won at competition or
- more social sources of incentive such as pleasing parents or attracting attention.

Intrinsic motivation sources include:

- excitement and enjoyment
- skills development and growth, a personal desire to learn
- overcoming challenges.

Obviously there is a role for extrinsic motivation sources such as the grading and belt progression in martial art training, and it can strengthen the intrinsic motivation that I want to cultivate in my students by adding to the excitement and challenge of training.

On the other hand, it can also weaken intrinsic motivation! The student who does not win a medal may feel demotivated or think that he is a failure. This will have a negative impact on his previous enjoyment of his training and may lead to quitting.

This is why I do not put students forward to grade for their next rank until I am confident that they will be successful. Where a student lacks any external motivation sources and is completely intrinsically motivated, he or she will not have the ambition or passion to become a champion, but that is not my goal.

My goal is to make a difference in the lives of my students and to give them tools that will help them throughout their lives.

So I really want to boost the students' intrinsic motivation and I believe that, as an instructor, I have a responsibility to provide the inspiration as well as teaching input that will do this.

Throughout this book I have highlighted a fact that I am sure is obvious to you, which is that every student is different. It goes without saying, then, that the things that motivate them are likely to be different.

What motivates one student will not motivate another so I need to know each student well enough to understand what motivates that particular individual. Only then can I provide a training environment that motivates, stimulates and rewards each student.

One of the things that will influence a student's motivation is the expectations that I levy on them. If my expectations are too low, the student may lower his performance level to meet my expectations. This will lead to boredom.

If my expectations are too high, the student is likely to see them as unachievable and a sense of defeat may cause them to lower their performance level. This may become a self-fulfilling prophecy in which the student fails to achieve and becomes discouraged and disillusioned with himself.

He/she may also become fearful about coming to class and quit suddenly or drift away slowly. Students will perform at their best when my expectations or targets are slightly above their present level of ability. They will rise to meet my expectations, increasing their self-confidence and spurring them on to greater efforts.

Another thing that motivates students to participate and to work their hardest is a sense of belonging. This is another reason why I make sure that all of my students know the history and traditions of their martial art. I want them to feel a sense of identity with those martial artists who created the art and started passing it on to others.

I also emphasize that the Institute is a community of learning, which everyone who joins my program belongs to – another reason why the Institute's image and identity is so important! The Institute consists of people from a range of ethnic backgrounds, different financial and social backgrounds, males, females, adults aged eighteen to sixty, children aged four and upwards, athletic people and the non-athletic, all different shapes and sizes. Now, anyone joining my program who has experienced a negative reaction to their ethnicity, size or personal circumstances will consciously or unconsciously be observing my verbal and non-verbal behavior towards them.

If they perceive any negative reaction or criticism on my part, they will never feel that sense of belonging, even if they persevere with the training. I treat every student the same and insist that my assistant instructors do the same.

I regularly tell them that my favorite students are those who put the most sweat on the floor. I see this as a way of promoting positive competition as well as reinforcing my often-expressed view that improvement is always possible for everyone.

Fear of failure is a fear that I have encountered in many students. They fear looking silly in front of others, letting people down, making mistakes. I have to show them that making mistakes is a way of learning. As long as we identify and correct the error then the error itself has been a positive thing not a negative one.

Shouting or laughing at a student, or allowing other students to laugh, will prevent them from trying the technique a second time, thus their growth is blighted. I try to create an environment where it is okay to make a mistake, what is not okay is not trying at all.

Although I have said that an element of competition can be helpful, I stress to my students the importance of self-comparison rather than comparison with others. I want them to focus on improving their own performance so that they each become their own personal best

Finally, what motivates me? I have said this many, many times. If I can make a difference in the life of just one person then my living will not have been in vain. Whatever I have achieved in my martial arts career and my professional career, nothing has given me a greater sense of achievement that seeing a student grow psychologically as well as physically to become a person with values and qualities that will help him or her to make a contribution to their community and to the world.

PART 3
APPLYING
LESSONS
LEARNED

THE TRADITIONAL TAEKWONDO INSTITUTE PROGRAM

Over the years I have found that the majority of students go on to university or college to complete their education. This includes adults!

A significant number of my adult students have undergraduate or advanced degrees, some of them having achieved these prior to joining the program and others having taken the decision, whilst in training, to return to college/ university to complete their education.

I cannot overestimate the value of a good education and it is never too late to learn. The process of getting an education and the process of earning a black belt are interlinked at the Institute.

I never get tired of telling my students that anyone can learn to kick and punch and that martial art training offers so much more to the student, but also places many demands on students physically, psychologically and philosophically, irrespective of age.

I want my students to be able to meet these demands so I provide a range of resources to support their learning. See Figure on next page:

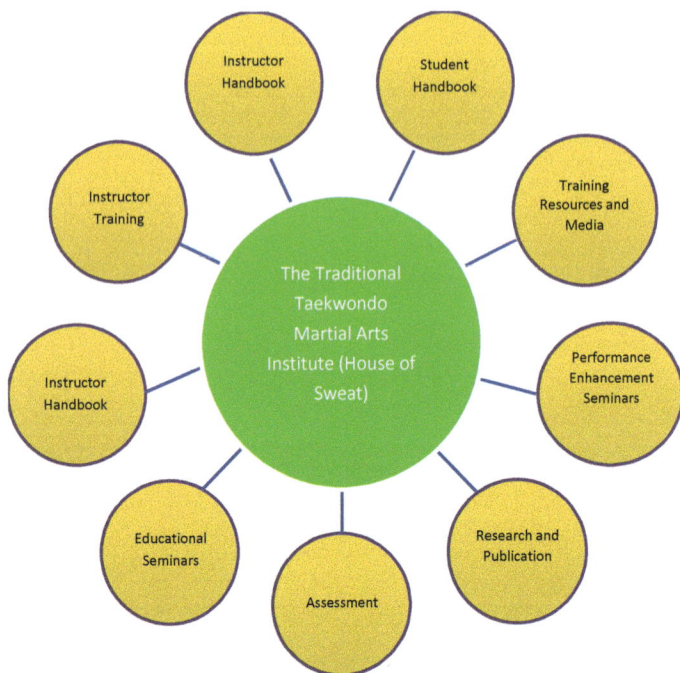

First of all, new students are given an information package, which contains the rules and regulations of the Institute, a vocabulary sheet with terms, phrases, the school motto and tenets of Taekwondo, and a DVD. The DVD shows them how to execute the first basic techniques so that they will be able to practise outwith class times from the very beginning. This welcoming DVD and information package supports the essential study habits required in both Taekwondo and higher education.

Just as school-age children have homework, my Taekwondo school expects its students to do homework and return to class showing that their learning has advanced.

In addition, the school has a student handbook (what learning centre do you know that does not have a manual for students?), and all students are expected to own their own copy of this. The Institute's student handbook provides the student with detailed information about history, customs and traditions; advanced vocabulary in Korean, Japanese and English; the school lineage and the syllabus for all belt levels up to fourth Dan. The overall purpose of this handbook is to provide the students with the information that enables them to create their own identity as practitioners within the global Taekwondo family. It encourages them to set their own goals and monitor their progress on the way to achieving the ultimate goal of becoming a black belt. This process is mirrored in their overall educational journey.

Grand Master Kwon taught me the benefits of using seminars to provide additional training and education, and I arrange two types of seminars for my students. The first is the educational seminar, which allows students to collect information on specific subject matter, e.g. the finer points of Poomsae presentation, the Hoshin Sool properties that are embedded in the Poomsae or Taekwondo developmental history.

This history also includes learning the Palgwes and about the various Kwans and their formation. Educational seminars create an environment that assists in physically and mentally challenging the students. The second type of seminar I organize is the performance enhancement seminar. The performance enhancement seminar has two primary functions.

Firstly, it allows the instructional staff to identify the inherent natural skills of the students. This helps us to create training packages to support their needs.

Secondly it provides students with the opportunity to receive instruction specifically tailored to their individual style as it applies to competing in national and international sporting events. The content of each seminar varies. Some are designed to improve agility, strength, coordination and conditioning, whilst others focus on tactics, strategies and situation drills. These seminars support the student's ability to reason, make sound decisions and stimulate quick-response thinking. There is still another advantage in hosting these performance seminars – it allows us to identify those students who have the potential for competing in international play.

In support of my conviction that there is much more to martial art than kicking and punching, our monitoring, measuring, testing and assessment procedures focus on the intellectual and emotional development of the student as well as on his/her technical skills development.

All students at the Institute are required to prepare an essay as part of their grading, so it's not just their physical skills being observed and monitored but their intellectual and emotional maturity.

We also evaluate a student's ability to take corrective action and to positively respond to criticism, and his or her ability to present and defend a logical argument.

The student's spirit and mindset are also important elements that need to be evaluated. How do we accomplish this? The yell, of course!

It's not just about breathing. The yell is the outward presentation of the student's mindset. A half-hearted yell is an indication of a student's less-than-committed attitude to what they are doing. This may be due to shyness or a lack of self-belief.

Yelling in the martial arts is developmental. In the beginning, first attempts are usually a faint sound that comes from the throat. As the student progresses, he or she learns that yelling tightens the abdominal muscles, making kicks and punches less painful.

He or she also finds that the yell improves focus and concentration. Eventually he or she will stop going home from class with a sore throat because their yell will come from the gut, not the throat.

A student's progress through all of these stages can be assessed and evaluated at each grading. Table 1 summarizes the expectations levied on students at each belt grading. They are not simply technical requirements. The mind is expected to develop in harmony with the body.

Table 1	Grading Requirements
Technical Requirements	Expectations
White Belt Given encouragement, praise and feedback; Mentorship.	Regular attendance, eager to learn, yell.
Yellow/Green Stripe Five to ten Kicks/Blocks associated with forms; Taeguek 1 and 2 or Palgwe 1 and 2; Kyukpa; Essay – What is Respect?/Ethics & Morality.	Have a little knowledge about rituals, customs, traditions, with less error; awareness of physical potential, yell.

Green/Blue Stripe Ten to fourteen Kicks/Blocks associated with forms; Taeguek 1 to 4 or Palgwe 1 to 4; Display Hoshin Sool & Gyoroogi; Kyukpa; Essay – What is TKD? / Tenets of TKD.	Beginning to see the tenets being applied and goal-setting; make historical connections.
Blue/Red Stripe Fourteen to nineteen Kicks/Blocks associated with forms; Taeguek 1 to 6 or Palgwe 1 to 6; Display Hoshin Sool and Gyoroogi; Kyukpa; Essay – TKD and the Non-violent Attitude/What is the Difference between a Leader and a Follower?	Tenets being applied, more goal-setting, judgement skills developing; self-awareness.
Black Belt Nineteen to twenty-five Kicks/Blocks associated with forms; Taeguek 1 to 7 or Palgwe 1 to 7; Display Hoshin Sool and Gyoroogi; Kyukpa; Essay – Diverse Culture/Why do we practice Poomsae?/What is a Black Belt?	Willingness to share with others, able to overcome challenges, find solutions to problems, correct errors using reasoning, be more observant and more responsible. The various stages of maturity should be evident at this point of the student's development (emotionally, intellectually, physically & philosophically).

To first Dan Twenty-five Kicks/Blocks associated with forms; Taeguek 1 to 8 **and** Palgwe 1 to 8; Display Hoshin Sool & Gyoroogi; Kyukpa; Essay – How can TKD help me in the future?/Roles and Responsibilities of a Black Belt/The History of Taekwondo.	Required to share with and give to others; demonstrate commitment and dedication, trustworthiness; greater understanding of self and values; spirit of humility – realizing he/she does not have all the answers; able to identify what needs to done and set a course of action.

I have always been interested in research into martial art and have participated in Kukkiwon's research program for a few years, with several papers being published. Now I know some of you reading this will be thinking that research is only for academics, but I couldn't disagree more. I'm sure every martial art instructor enthuses about the psychological and physical benefits of martial art training but I think it is crucial to have evidence to support these claims rather than rhetoric alone. Research helps us to understand why some of our teaching techniques work and others fail dismally. It challenges us to look at ourselves in the mirror of other people's eyes and to reassess what and how we teach so that the needs and expectations of today's students are being met. I began my martial art training fifty-three years ago. The way I was taught was the norm for those days but times have changed and I cannot base my teaching approach solely on my own experience of learning. If I did, students would not stay!

This may seem to be contradictory to my stance as a traditional martial art instructor but I would argue that traditions are dynamic rather than static. They contain some of the best ideas of our predecessors in martial art and should not be discarded as inappropriate for the modern world. Respecting and honoring traditions gives students a feeling of belonging. I know this because my research has generated evidence that this is the case. It connects all of us with our history and helps to keep our lineage stable and strong. Upholding traditions does not prevent growth and development in martial art; rather, it provides a solid foundation on which to build.

Good martial art etiquette is one of the traditions that I uphold. Demonstrating respect for the martial art and the instructors who are teaching you will increase the student's respect for himself and others, and this attitude will affect all aspects of an individual's life. This is discipline at work!

This reminds me of one of my classes with Hanshi Hargrove. It was his custom to start each class with a run. This run varied between two and five miles. One late afternoon during the spring, Hanshi decided to conduct the class on the beach. This was both for advertisement and for a change in the training environment. It probably reminded him of days training in Okinawa. In Okinawa the teacher always carried a stick, which he used to motivate and stimulate the students. Hanshi had adopted this practice.

I had the unfortunate 'pleasure' of being positioned in rank in front of some dead debris that had been washed up on the beach. The debris was covered with flies! My movement performing kicking and punching drills attracted flies to my sweaty face. A couple of flies became infatuated with my sweaty face and began to walk across it, across my forehead, my chin, my eyes! One flew away and the other remained. I dared not fan it away because Hanshi was directly behind me with the stick and his command was to punch, not to fan flies. The fly somehow worked its way under my right nostril. I sucked it up as I was chambering my right hand, preparing to punch, and blew it out of my mouth as I executed the punch. The fly was gone and I didn't get hit by the stick! The lesson here is learning not to be distracted by minor irritations.

Discipline is instilled in all of the students as they grow and develop through the ranks. Another sign of discipline at work is students' use of title to address senior students and instructors. To this day I never call any of my instructors by anything other than their martial title.

All senior students and all instructors have titles and I insist that these are used at all times. Students are required to bow and to greet the instructor when entering and leaving the dojang. Each class begins with a call to attention and bow to the instructor and ends with a repetition of the tenets of Taekwondo, the school's motto and a bow to the instructors who have taught the class. The call to attention and the formal bows must also be observed by any other students who are watching the class; leaning against a wall at these times is forbidden.

Blind obedience on the part of students is not something I demand, and indeed, it would be potentially dangerous for the student to internalize such an attitude. I explain why the tradition is important and how the whole school benefits from observing it. I am always clear that it is not a deep bow, as one would use when bowing to Allah, rather it is a sign of respect. This respect should also be shown to classmates before and after practice or sparring. No one is permitted to enter my dojang unless they have first removed their shoes. Students should be wearing a clean dobok and there should be no smell that indicates they have been smoking or drinking before coming to class. 'Chit-chat' or whispering to one another during training is also not tolerated and I impress on students the necessity of focus and concentration as well as respect. All instructors must be treated with respect and addressed by their title e.g. 'Sabum Nim' or as 'Sir' or 'Miss/Ma'am'.

My classes are taught in the Korean language and include the practice of basic combat techniques: jireugi (punching), maki (blocking), chagi (kicking) and chigi (striking). Mastery of the basics is crucial, as I have said elsewhere in this book! Students often tell me that they really enjoy having a new white belt student in the class as this gives them the opportunity to focus on the fundamentals and make some improvements in their performance. Occasionally students leave a few weeks after joining because they are still working on basic blocks and kicks and have not been taught jumping or flying kicks. They expect instant gratification of their desires and are simply not prepared to spend years of their life learning the art. These are not the students I want in my program and I would never consider compromising the integrity of the art for the sake of money.

Time after time I stress to my students that martial art is not a game. It must be taken seriously. Whilst I appeal to every student to practise at home, I absolutely forbid them to attempt to perform any technique that they have not been taught by an instructor in the class, and no student must ever attempt to teach other students, either in class or outwith class, without my permission.

THE LEGACY

The WTF has done an excellent job of promoting Taekwondo as a competitive and worldwide Olympic sport.

However, there is enough evidence to support the argument that the sport has become too elitist, far beyond the physical skill and interest of the average Taekwondo practitioner globally. From a poll that I carried out with my students, I was able to identify the main reasons why they had started Taekwondo training. Those reasons were:

1. to be able to defend themselves
2. to get into good physical shape
3. to develop discipline.

No one mentioned a desire to get involved in competition activities!

As a traditionalist, I place my teaching emphasis on self-defence, although I do teach the sport and those of my students who compete have been very successful. That's as it should be: the sport should be a part of martial art training, but only a part. Martial art is a way of life!

It is estimated that over eighty million people practise Taekwondo. It is also estimated that only about eight million will ever enter the competition ring. This means that approximately seventy-two million, or ninety percent, do not compete. Even the Republic of South Korea has noted a decline in Taekwondo interest. The majority of people who practise Taekwondo do it for the physical, emotional and spiritual benefits that are traditionally associated with classic Taekwondo. Classic Taekwondo focuses on its students and the development of the whole person, in order that they become responsible individuals who are willing to serve their God and their country, and help their neighbors.

It is very disturbing to me and, I know, to many of you reading this book, that sport Taekwondo now dominates the Korean scene and there is a real risk that the traditional 'martial' component will be lost. My concern about the loss of the 'martial' aspect of Taekwondo led to my setting up a Global Task Group of Masters and Grand Masters from six continents dedicated to the preservation of Taekwondo, the martial art: 'The Lost Product'. I am firmly of the opinion that it is the 'martial' characteristic of the art, as opposed to the sporting aspect, which has resulted in the positive behavioral and psychological developments that I have observed in numerous students over the years, and it would be wrong to allow this to disappear.

I set about creating the Global Task Group in 2012. It is an organization made up of Taekwondo Masters and Grand Masters from all over the world who are focused on the preservation of Taekwondo the martial art. Its objective is to offer training and certification in martial Taekwondo (Mudo), rather than the sport of Taekwondo.

If this sounds like a radical step, I am happy. The actions required to sustain and promote Taekwondo as a martial art, rather than a sport, must be revolutionary in that they should reflect western needs, values and culture.

I have a vision of recapturing 'The Lost Product' (namely Taekwondo the martial art), hence the GTG. After three years' hard work and many setbacks and hurdles to be overcome, I have succeeded in having a conference to plan the work that the GTG needs to carry out.

Whilst the WTF will continue to lead the sporting component of Taekwondo and the educational sector, the GTG will take the global lead in preserving the traditional martial art of Taekwondo that stresses the development of the individual within a family of Taekwondo practitioners.

Unfortunately, the Kukkiwon's services have been reduced to Dan Certification only. Under the present cloud of controversy, many MASTERS on the world stage have decided to discontinue using Kukkiwon's services.

My plan for the GTG is that it will offer a number of training seminars that will attract and be attended by Taekwondo practitioners and Taekwondo MASTERS globally throughout the year and for the years to come. Again, these will have western influences and western ideas reflecting western culture.

Now I expect some of you are holding up your hands in horror at the thought of such momentous changes and I can understand this! Think about it though. Are you really so committed to allowing Taekwondo to become a sport for only elite athletes? I think what people tend to be afraid of is not the change itself but the path to the change – that place in between, where we have to let go and trust in ourselves. For change to happen there has to be a shared vision and I have shared this with many of you face to face, through my website, via email and telephone calls. Now I am sharing it in this book.

Change for the sake of change can be disastrous, I agree, and change that takes place overnight will not be sustainable. There needs to be a compelling need and that compelling need is the need to have a martial art legacy to pass on to those who will come after us. Finally, it can't be just a pipe dream. There needs to be a practical way of achieving the vision, in other words – the GTG.

BUDDHIST PHILOSOPHY

Zen has profoundly influenced the development of martial arts like Kendo (Kenjutsu), Kyudo (Kyujutsu), Judo (Jujutsu), Karate, Aikido and Taekwondo.

In ancient Japan, Zen had a major impact on Samurai warriors, and it was widely adopted as their official religion. The Samurai achieved perfection in martial arts such as Kenjutsu, Kyujutsu, and Jujutsu through the practice of Zazen (seated meditation).

The practice of Zen was ideal for the Samurai way of life as it put emphasis on self-composure, vigilance, and tranquility in the face of death.

Many people in the Western world practise martial arts as a sport, without the spirit of Zen as their foundation, for obvious reasons.

It is neither necessary nor sufficient for the typical martial arts instructor to have a comprehensive understanding of philosophical concepts and ideas in order to teach or have a successful program with prospective students. Nor is an understanding of the mystic phenomena, as it applies to the kicking and punching art, required.

Buddhist principles are deeply embedded within nearly every part of the training. Whether it be stretching exercises, conditioning calisthenics or applying combative manipulation strategies, the Buddhist principles and practices are at work.

Sensitivities to philosophical preferences have the potential to give rise to debate and conflict, therefore we at the Institute subscribe to keeping it simple, confining these ancient practices to just quotations and phrases, e.g.

"A journey of a thousand miles begins with the first step," or "Man's mind is like the roots of a tree. It will absorb everything around it, even the poison that will kill it."

Both quotes are from the *Kung Fu* TV series. When I was younger I watched this weekly series on TV. These two statements made such an impact on me that I have never forgotten them and through the years I regularly quote them to my students.

However, an applied understanding of the concept of the "Five Minds" is appropriate, adaptable and very easy to implement into anyone's program. These 'Minds' were briefly introduced earlier.

They are:

Shoshin (this concept in Zen Buddhism means 'beginner's mind')

The state of shoshin is that of a beginner's mind. The shoshin mind allows you to maintain the attitude that everything is new. It is a mistake in martial art training to start to think that you have 'got it' and there is nothing more to learn. Keep the white belt eagerness to learn throughout your training.

Hanshi would periodically say to us, "Don't expect me to teach you everything. You must steal the techniques for yourselves – make them yours." This means that the student must play an active role in every class, seeing with a shoshin mind, in order to steal the essence of each day's lesson.

ZANSHIN (LINGERING MIND)

This mind is the state of total alertness, awareness of your surroundings and readiness for action. You are focused on the technique you are implementing before, during and after you have implemented it.

MUSHIN (NO MIND)

Mushin is defined to be "No mind, a mind without ego. A mind like a mirror which reflects and does not judge." The original term was "mushin no shin", meaning, "mind of no mind." It is a state of mind without fear, anger, or anxiety. Once you have mastered a technique, you can execute it without thinking.

FUDOSHIN (IMMOVABLE MIND)

An unshakable mind and an immovable spirit is the state of fudoshin. The mind is without fear and completely at peace. Nothing can alarm this mind and any situation can be faced with serenity.

SENSHIN (PURIFIED SPIRIT; ENLIGHTENED ATTITUDE)

Senshin is the unity of mind and spirit. Senshin is a spirit of compassion that wishes to do no harm to anyone. It holds all life to be sacred. It is the Buddha mind and its perception is the path to the 'Do ('the way' of the empty hand and foot).

Shoshin can heighten a student's awareness of the world around him or her, thus offering the opportunity to rediscover and discover sights and sounds and other things to see what he/she would not have seen before.

Zanshin can increase the student's total awareness of how and when to apply techniques during self-defence drills (hoshin sool) and sparring training (kumite or gyoroogi).

Mushin can eliminate a student's nervousness or self-induced stress when put in a situation that demands calmness and self-control. Successfully applied, it often leads to better performance.

Fudoshin can also be called 'indomitable spirit, which is one of the five tenets of Taekwondo. A never-quit attitude.

Senshin can only be achieved through years of continuous training with the direct supervision of your teacher. Attaining this mental state indicates that you have a complete understanding of your martial art, what you are doing, and why! Most martial artists never reach this level because it transcends beyond the physical and has become internal.

Incorporating the concept of these five elements is a must for the serious martial artist. They are very valuable tools that will assist in your personal development and growth, both inside and outside of the dojang/dojo.

And teaching these concepts does not require that the master instructor be a scholar. Keep it simple.

MEDITATION (MUK NYUM IN KOREAN, MOKUSŌ IN JAPANESE)

The tool for centuries that has been used to ease a racing mind or to analyze a subject under study has been meditation or contemplation. The practice of meditation particularly applies to the early days of my martial arts training.

Each and every class ended in meditation, a moment of quiet, of peace, to rest the mind, to reflect; sometimes contemplating on what was taught and sometimes reflecting on what has been learned. Or just simply trying to make a connection with where you are and where you would like to be.

The meditation time varied each time – sometimes five minutes, sometimes ten. No one to my knowledge noticed the time span. The workout was so hard that I think we all looked forward to meditation time.

At the sound of the word "Mokuso" shouted out, usually by the most senior student in class, I would slowly close my eyes and drift off to no particular place, no particular thought.

I allowed my mind to take me where it wanted to go.

I was told once that the mind should not be in any particular place. So I never tried to direct the sight of my mind's eye. Rather, I focused on my breathing. Each time I inhaled deeper and deeper, completely filling my lungs with fresh oxygen.

And each time I exhaled, I could feel bits of effort exiting my body until I was completely relaxed, totally free of any effort.

Inhaling gently in the nose and softly out of the mouth, over and over and over again, until I lost connection with my immediate surroundings.

Piercing through my effortless drifting, through a space of nothingness, I faintly hear "Mokuso Ni Re," as the sign that meditation ends.

Sometimes the focus was on the breathing. With us all sitting on the floor in perfect posture, Mr Hankins would clap his hands together, which was the signal for us to start inhaling, and we inhaled until he clapped his hands again which signalled us to start exhaling. The time-spacing between the claps grew longer and longer. So we learned how to inhale longer and to exhale nearly twice as long. Grand Master Lee did something similar.

About five or six years ago, the respiratory department of the Aberdeen hospital conducted a breathing test on me. My lung capacity test results were off the scales, in spite of having suffered from asthma. I attribute this to my martial arts training and those breathing exercises.

CLOSING THOUGHTS

Serving as both a role model in the martial arts of Okinawan Shorin-Ryu Karate and WTF Taekwondo, and as a mentor who inspires and encourages people to operate out of their comfort-zone solely for the purpose of getting the best out of an individual, is a tradition dating back several centuries; delicately handed down from father to son; master to student.

The very inception of martial arts training focused on the improvement in quality of life for those who followed the 'Do'.

I have often stated to my students that:

"Any idiot can learn to kick and punch. So there must be something more to martial arts training."

I haven't found out exactly what makes successful development and growth for those who enter our training programs, but at the Institute, we continue to make a conscientious effort to replicate exactly what has been handed down from my teacher, my teacher's teacher and his teacher's teacher, while employing very little intervention.

As mentioned earlier, I have been with my Karate teacher for forty-two years and my Taekwondo teacher, thirty-three. My Karate teacher has been with his teacher for fifty-plus years. Three generations of martial arts instructors who are, to date, still alive.

The Institute has an incredible resource-base, which allows continuity, accuracy, correctness and clarity in areas of uncertainty.

Three generations offering visible evidence of personal success stories covering the globe of life-changing characteristics that can be directly linked to martial arts training, when taught by knowledgeable, well-taught and dedicated teachers.

MY TEACHERS

GM Jung Un Lee

GM Duk Gun Kwon

GM Hankins

GM Frank Hargrove

GM Hae Man Park

Gyokusui Toyoaki Niina gosoke

THE INSTITUTE'S INSTRUCTOR STAFF

All Institute Staff have passed instructor training and are Kukkiwon and Okinawan Shorin-ryu Karate ranked

TESTIMONIALS

Mrs Nazia Shafi of Aberdeen, Scotland wrote on
19 December 2015

*(Three of her children train at the Institute; two are
International Champions.)*

Kwan Jang Nim

Martial arts training has had a hugely positive impact on
my children. They have been training for over ten years and
have learnt the importance of discipline, commitment, respect,
hard work and perseverance. This has influenced them in their
school environment and their approach to studying.

Their commitment to martial arts formed a major part
of their personal statements for university applications. This
was important and seen as a great advantage. It made them
stand out from the crowd as it showed that they were willing
to commit, work hard and not give up easily, especially as
nowadays it is all too easy to lose interest in things quickly.
They have learnt skills that they will take with them wherever
they go, and hopefully pass onto others, no matter what the
future holds for them.

Pu Sabum Kris Morrison of Peterhead, Scotland –
now living in the USA wrote on 20 December 2015

(Three-events gold-medallist International Champion)

This year marks the twentieth year that I have been training in Taekwondo, which equates to almost two-thirds of my lifetime thus far. Without martial arts, and Taekwondo specifically, I strongly believe I would be a much lesser person and would have achieved much less in life.

One particular period in my life sticks out. Around 2003 I was not enjoying University and was strongly considering whether I should even complete the degree. Grand Master Harrell, along with support from my parents and grandparents, were key to me finishing University by constantly reinforcing the message that an education was critical to succeed in life – Kwan Jang Nim often reiterated the phrase "A mind is a terrible thing to waste." The dojang became a sanctuary to forget about everything else going on; I persevered and graduated in 2005.

By completing this education a number of doors were opened to me, allowing me to live and work in Greece, London, New York, Los Angeles and now Palm Springs, California where I am now married and together we have three beautiful boys. I still train in Taekwondo multiple times per week and recently my four-year-old has joined me in training. Without martial arts and the influence of Grand Master Harrell, life may have been very different.

Martial arts are much more than simply kicking and punching; it may be cliched but they are truly a 'Way of Life'.

I wish Grand Master Harrell every success with his book.

Master Margaret Evans of Ellon, Scotland wrote
on 20 December 2015

*(Instructional Staff member, three-events gold-medallist
International Champion)*

Martial art training has had an enormous impact on my life.
When I first started twelve years ago it was just on a whim as
I had a very sedentary lifestyle. I did not expect to ever reach
black belt or to change in any way, except perhaps to become
physically fitter. Nonetheless it has had a profound effect
on how other people view me and how I view myself. Work
colleagues regard me with surprise and a new respect when
they discover about my martial art training. I now have the
confidence to attempt tasks in the dojang and in my day-to-
day life that I would previously have said were far out with my
physical and mental capabilities. The structure and discipline
of the classes has given me the motivation and determination
to work to improve my health and physical fitness, to strive
to increase my knowledge and skill, and to make the most
of the opportunities that each day brings. I have learned that
my perceived limitations have been self-imposed and can be
overcome through perseverance and this gives me a tremendous
sense of achievement. I have learned that it is okay to fall down
so long as I get back up and try again.

Martial art training has also given me access to a culture,
tradition and heritage which I am proud and privileged to be
part of. I am committed to contributing what I can to ensuring
that the traditions are passed onto the next generation so that
others can receive the benefits that I have gained.

LINZY MILLER SHERRIFF OF ABERDEEN, SCOTLAND WROTE
ON 22 DECEMBER 2015

(British National Team, two times, two-events gold-medallist International Championship)

Taekwondo has impacted on my life greatly. I started Taekwondo at the Traditional Taekwondo Institute at the age of fourteen and through my training under Grand Master Harrell, it has helped me focus on what is important while being able to ignore any distractions.

It has transformed me mentally and physically.

The structure and discipline of Taekwondo, I feel, has made me a better person and I've learned to always look for ways to improve myself regardless of how difficult it may seem. The benefits gained include flexibility, strength, speed and endurance.

The biggest impact it has given me is the realization that I am in complete control of my life. Any changes or desires I wanted to achieve were achievable if I took responsibility.

With this in mind I went on to study nursing at university and have now been a qualified nurse for eleven years. Also mentoring students and newly qualified nurses.

Taekwondo has allowed me to grow in self-confidence. I have learned to use courtesy, to give and earn respect. To speak respectfully to instructors and students and encourage and expand upon the skills and knowledge they have.

Taekwondo is about succeeding. There is no giving up, so there is no failing.

It is not about learning faster than others or being better than others, but about becoming a better you.

PU SABUM JOHN DICKIE OF ELLON, SCOTLAND WROTE ON
22 DECEMBER 2015

*(Instructional Staff member, three-events gold-medallist
International Champion)*

In general terms, Taekwondo has given me a higher level of
fitness, confidence, flexibility, ability to defend myself etc.

In more recent years I have developed the awareness to
apply the training and skills outside the confines of the actual
classes themselves.

Almost four years ago in a restructure by the bank I lost my
position as a Commercial Business Manager. I was unemployed
and had only three months to find another position within the
bank

I was successful in redeploying into a new role as a Private
Relationship Manager. Confidence and working conditions
within the organization were at a low point due to number of
job losses and changes in culture and procedures.

Within twelve months of taking on the role I was basically
told by my line manager that I should seek employment
outside of the bank as he did not see me as part of his team
going forward.

At this low point I sat down and decided to approach the
issues from a martial arts perspective and apply my training to
solving work issues.

As a result of addressing all issues in this way, I completed
a transformation in which, for the last two years, I have been
viewed as a role model. I received a behavioral rating very
seldom given within the bank, and this was the only time I

had achieved this within the bank. The rating was given by the same manager who, at one time, thought I should move on.

It has also helped me facilitate a move from Aberdeen to Edinburgh.

HASHIM ZAIN ALZAABI OF SHARJAH, UNITED ARAB EMIRATES, WROTE ON 25 DECEMBER 2015

In this generation we are always busy with life and easily distracted by life activities (study, work, personal problems, etc.). Training in general and martial arts in particular offers a unique solution through its training program which I found very effective and useful. I gained many skills while training, including the ability to free my mind from daily schedules, and reenergize my body.

SUN BAE ALI AL FARAI TRAINED AT THE INSTITUE WHILE ATTENDING ABERDEEN COLLEGE – NOW BACK HOME IN MUSCAT, OMAN, WROTE ON 26 DECEMBER 2015

In the past, I used to be very weak physically and in my personality. I used to be afraid of walking alone. When I learned martial arts, I felt peaceful. I didn't have that fear anymore. I gained not just physical strength but also strength in my personality. I became a different person, a better person.

When I was trained by Kwan Jang Nim, he taught me what a real martial artist is and that we must not forget the tradition and the origin of it. He also taught me to be myself. Martial art is a journey that is worth the taking.

Pu Sabum Elliot Thornton from Ellon, Scotland, now six years with British Armed Forces, wrote on 26 December 2015

(Three-events gold-medallist International Champion)

How has martial arts training impacted my life?

Profoundly; before I had martial arts I did not realize it. But after, I started to utilize martial arts training in all aspects of my life, and not just the physical. Now I cannot conceive of a life without martial arts.

Martial arts makes you a better person and, properly applied, makes better every endeavor you choose.

All this is, of course, only possible when the martial arts are properly taught.

Jorge G. Mirabal (one of my first students 1977) of New Jersey, USA – wrote on 1 January 2016

How have the martial arts impacted me?

For one, it has made me wiser, more considerate of others, more humility and understanding of others and what karate really is… most of all, peace of mind.

JYO KYO HAMED AL DHAHRI TRAINED AT THE INSTITUE
WHILE STUDYING AT ABERDEEN UNIVERSITY – NOW BACK
HOME IN MUSCAT, OMAN, WROTE ON 2 JANUARY 2016

Martial arts has positively impacted my life, Al-hamdulillah. I learned that results come after effort and that persistence and consistency are vital for progress. I learned that our biggest obstacles lie within us and not in outer circumstance and that, with Allah's help, no hurdle is too big to overcome.

PROF. ARTHUR L. RIZER III (MY FIRST NATIONAL
CHAMPION 1994) LAW PROFESSOR AT THE UNIVERSITY OF
WEST VIRGINIA, USA – WROTE ON 2 JANUARY 2016

How has martial arts training impacted my life? It's hard to answer this question without using clichés, e.g. it changed my life, made me the man I am today… but the truth is it did change my life and it did help me become the man I am today.

I met Kyoshi, officially known to me then as David Harrell, but in my heart he will forever be Sabum-Nim, when I was thirteen. I was a struggling young man. I was a terrible student, and that is being kind, I had incredibly low self-esteem. I was both bullied and a bully to those smaller than me – in fact I was given the option to either join Sabum-Nim's Taekwondo (TKD) class or be suspended for picking on a fellow student (who was, of course, smaller than me). I was terrified that I would not be able to go to college due to my grades and I was further terrified that I would grow up to be a man that neither my family nor I could be proud of. That was my starting point.

I trained in TKD for five years – reaching first Dan at the age of eighteen. TKD taught me how to be both a leader but also how to follow. I first used those skills as the co-captain for the Washington State Jr. Olympic Team where I took second in state and then third in the national competition. I further used those skills after I joined the United States Army rising from the ranks of Private to Sergeant and then Lieutenant to Lieutenant Colonel when I retired after twenty years of service, earning the Bronze Star and Purple Heart medal during my combat deployment to Iraq.

TKD promoted my self-esteem, confidence, and discipline. Skills that I used to become a solid student who received a full ROTC scholarship to college and then graduated magna cum laude from Gonzaga University Law School and then with distinction with my advanced law degree from Georgetown University Law Center. It is the same skills that I am using twenty years after I received my black belt to attend Oxford University while I finish up my DPhil (PhD) with the Faculty of Law.

Now, at the age of thirty-nine, twenty-six years after I first walked into the cafeteria that served as Sabum-Nim's dojang, I have my dream job – a tenured tracked law school professor, an author who has written three books, and most importantly a father – whose first-born son is a first Dan black belt. So yes, it is a cliché, but martial arts training led me to the man I am – it changed my life.

Gamal Mahdi, MD, of Aberdeen, Scotland wrote on 4 January 2016

Reflections on the impact of martial arts training programme by a parent of four children who took part in Mr David J. Harrell's training:

I have known Mr Harrell for almost thirteen years, and our four children have cumulatively undergone training in David's different martial arts programmes for close to twenty years between them all. Each and every one of our children has been touched by this outstanding personality and his classes. As a family, we have come to the realization that martial arts training and our children's achievement in it, has become an important positive aspect of our family's life. I find it difficult to put into words the impact this training has had, although I can say that martial arts training with David is a way of life for trainees, like our children. Such as the way it sets a dynamic routine and engrains self-discipline into them. The usual struggle of time management and prioritization of tasks, which they have had to learn how to deal with, is an example. The two prominent intellectual faculties I feel trainees are encouraged to practise, besides and equally importantly as the physical skills, are patience and respect – patience in learning new skills, perseverance, tolerance and adaptation. Respect for themselves, their families, their teachers, their community and moreover, for their own and for others' beliefs. Our family's journey with martial arts and David Harrell started with us attempting to achieve a modest goal of building our children's self-confidence in today's potentially physically hostile environment. After all these years we realized that David's students do not only achieve that self-confidence, but they learn a lot about sharing, compassion, leadership and modesty.

Needless to say that the sole and lead founder of the program in Aberdeen, David Harrell, has drafted and developed it over the years in a unique and assertive style. Again, it is difficult to put in words some of the features of this style. Suffice to say that David with his palpable sincerity and warmth, and with his tireless devotion to his art and his students, teaches leadership in martial arts by giving a live example of what moral leadership should be.

ABOUT THE AUTHOR

GM David J. Harrell, a graduate from Norfolk State University, has had a successful career as an Electrical Marine Designer, Nuclear Power Station Design and an Aerospace Electrical Design Engineer while holding an eighth Dan in WTF Taekwondo, a seventh Dan in Okinawan Shorin-Ryu Karate, a fourth Dan in Hapkido, fifth Dan in Gumdo, second Dan rank in Ryu Kyu Kobudo and second Dan Mugairyu Iaido.

GM Harrell has made presentations at Kukkiwon sponsored Leaders Forums, Symposiums hosted by the Taekwondo Promotion Foundation/University of California Berkeley, and has had his research studies published by the Kukkiwon Research Institute of Taekwondo. More recently, GM Harrell participated in the 19th Kukkiwon Poomsae/Dan Promotion Test Examiner Course held in Chicago Illinois, USA, from November 19 to 22, 2015.

Grand Master Harrell, the father of three teenage sons and two adult daughters and a grandfather of five, has been practising martial arts for more than fifty-three years. His training dates back to the early 1960s.

He opened his first commercial school site on October 13, 1991, after years of teaching at the Junior High School in the city of Federal Way, Washington. This program would produce twenty-five black belters.

He moved to Aberdeen, Scotland in 1998 and established the first WTF Taekwondo program in the north-east of Scotland. GM Harrell has three Taekwondo schools in the greater Aberdeen area.

To date:

- 118 black belts (93 in Scotland)
- 72 Students with Undergraduate degrees
- 12 Students with Masters Degrees
- 7 Students with PhDs
- 27 International Champions
- 16 National Champions
- 27 Regional Champions
- 1 Student on the British National Team (while earning a BSc Degree).

Students at the Institute are truly armed with productive thinking skills as a direct result of the inherent educational content of martial art training coupled with the teaching approach offered.

He is passionate in his belief that traditional martial art training leads to positive personal development, physically, psychologically and philosophically, irrespective of age of the practitioner.

The martial art that Grand Master Harrell teaches his students is that same martial art that he was taught by his own instructors because he knows that it works! It makes a difference in the lives of those who practise it.

GM Harrell is concerned about the direction that

Taekwondo seems to be taking and feels most strongly that change is urgently needed. Sport Taekwondo now dominates the Korean Taekwondo scene, and that sport has become too elitist, far beyond the physical skill and interest of the average Taekwondo practitioner.

There is a real risk that the traditional 'martial' component will be lost and there will be no Taekwondo martial art legacy to pass on to the next generation. The loss of the 'martial' aspect of Taekwondo has been a source of concern to Grand Master Harrell for many years, and is the driving force behind the writing of this book as well as the creation of the Global Task Group Ltd (GTG), which is dedicated to the preservation of Taekwondo, the martial art.

He refers to this situation as 'The Lost Product'.

Today, the GTG is in a position to provide training that will support the modern instructional needs of today's Masters, while creating meaningful direction for future generations in the preservation of Taekwondo, the martial art.

GM Harrell's teaching philosophy and training approach are reflected throughout the pages of this book.

GM David J. Harrell CEO
www.globaltaskgroup.org
www.wtf-scotland.com
+44 (0) 7803 897422 mob
1 (734) 418-9394 (free call from USA & Canada)

GENO CHART – SHURI-TE / SHORIN-RYU

As of Sept. 29, 2015

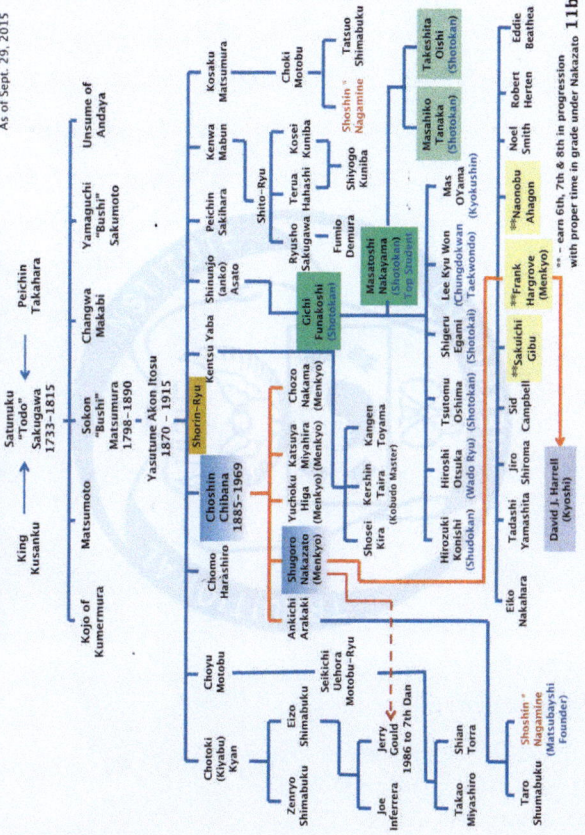

King Kusanku

Satunuku "Todo" Sakugawa 1733–1815

Sokon "Bushi" Matsumura 1798–1890

Yasutune Akon Itosu 1870 - 1915

Matsumoto

Kojo of Kumermura

Chomo Hanashiro

Choshin Chibana 1885–1969

Shorin-Ryu

Kentsu Yaba

Changwa Makabi

Yamaguchi "Bushi" Sakumoto

Peichin Takahara

Unsume of Andaya

Kosaku Matsumura

Choki Motobu

Tatsuo Shimabuku

Shinunjo (anko) Asato

Gichin Funakoshi (Shotokan)

Peichin Sakihara

Kenwa Mabun

Shito-Ryu

Terua Hahashi

Kosei Kuniba

Shiyogo Kuniba

Shoshin ° Nagamine

Takeshita Oishi (Shotokan)

Masahiko Tanaka (Shotokan)

Ryusho Sakugawa

Fumio Demura

Masatoshi Nakayama (Shotokan) Top Student

Mas OYama (Kyokushin)

Ankichi Arakaki

Shugoro Nakazato (Menkyo)

Yuchoku Higa (Menkyo)

Katsuya Miyahira (Menkyo)

Chozo Nakama (Menkyo)

Kangen Toyama

Shosei Kira

Kershin Taira (Kobudo Master)

Hiroshi Otsuka (Wado Ryu)

Tsutomu Oshima (Shotokan)

Shigeru Egami (Shotokan)

Lee Kyu Won (Chungdokwan) Taekwondo)

Hirozuki Konishi (Shudokan)

Jiro Campbell

Sid Campbell

Sakuichi Gibu

**Frank Hargrove (Menkyo)

**Naonobu Ahagon

Tadashi Yamashita Shiroma

David J. Harrell (Kyoshi)

Eiko Nakahara

Noel Smith

Robert Herten

Eddie Beathea

Choyu Motobu

Chotoki (Kiyabu) Kyan

Eizo Shimabuku

Seikichi Uehora Motobu-Ryu

Jerry Gould 1986 to 7th Dan

Zenryo Shimabuku

Joe Inferrera

Shian Torra

Takao Miyashiro

Taro Shumabuku

Shoshin ° Nagamine (Matsubayshi Founder)

** - earn 6th, 7th & 8th in progression with proper time in grade under Nakazato

11b